TO RN

TO RN

Embracing the
New Covenant in an
Old Covenant World

MIKE MANUEL

Trilogy Christian Publishers A Wholly Owned Subsidiary of Trinity Broadcasting Network 2442 Michelle Drive Tustin, CA 92780

Copyright © 2020 Mike Manuel

Rights Department, 2442 Michelle Drive, Tustin, CA 92780.

Trilogy Christian Publishing/ TBN and colophon are trademarks of Trinity Broadcasting Network.

For information about special discounts for bulk purchases, please contact Trilogy Christian Publishing.

Trilogy Disclaimer: The views and content expressed in this book are those of the author and may not necessarily reflect the views and doctrine of Trilogy Christian Publishing or the Trinity Broadcasting Network.

Manufactured in the United States of America

10 9 8 7 6 5 4 3 2 1

Library of Congress Cataloging-in-Publication Data is available.

B-ISBN#: 978-1-64773-186-1

E-ISBN#: 978-1-64773-187-8

ACKNOWLEDGEMENTS

First and foremost, I want to acknowledge the Holy Spirit for His work in guiding me and illuminating God's Word to me. I want to thank my friend, JC Ellender, for his encouragement in my life and in the writing of this book. Thanks also to my wife, Donna, for her support and encouragement. I also want to acknowledge Sarah Ebersole for her help in editing this manuscript. And finally, a big thanks to the great people who make up the local church that I pastor. They have not only graciously given me the time to work on this book but have also been a constructive sounding board for the ideas and concepts presented in *TORN*.

TABLE OF CONTENTS

INTRODUCTION

Much of Jesus' earthly ministry centered around His announcement that He was ushering in the kingdom of God and a brand-new agreement between God and mankind, known as the New Covenant. This New Covenant was not simply a series of amendments to the 1,500-year-old Old Covenant, but rather an entirely new agreement that changed just about everything for God's people.

Some responded very favorably to this new way of doing things and quickly embraced the New Covenant. Others, however, found Jesus' new way of doing things offensive and even threatening to their current lifestyle. Another group of people embraced many aspects of the New Covenant, yet still held onto many rituals and traditions from the Old Covenant.

In a somewhat cryptic parable, Jesus warned against trying to mix the Old and New Covenants.

No one sews a patch of unshrunk cloth on an old garment, for the patch will pull away from the garment, making the tear worse. Neither do people pour new wine into old wineskins. If they do, the skins will burst; the wine will run out and the wineskins will be ruined. No, they pour new wine into new wineskins, and both are preserved.
Matthew 9:16-17 NIV

In this parable, the Old Covenant is represented by an old garment that has a hole in it. If you patch it with a new piece of material, the new material will shrink when washed and will actually tear the garment as it shrinks. If you were wondering where the title for this book came from, now you know. *Torn.*

Torn, because so many of us are trying to mix the new with the old. Jesus didn't come to patch up the Old Covenant, because a patch wouldn't fix it. It would actually make it worse. He came with a brand-new covenant.

In this same parable, Jesus also uses the illustration of putting new wine into old wineskins. New wine continues to ferment and to give off gas for quite some time. An old wineskin has already been stretched as far as it will stretch, so when it's filled with new wine, there's no stretch left for the expanding gases of the new wine. So, if you make the mistake of putting new wine into an old wineskin, it's going to tear and you're going to have a mess. *Torn.* Torn, because we're trying to mix the new with the old.

Two thousand years after the initiation of the New Covenant, many Christians are still clinging to several of the rituals and traditions of the Old Covenant while trying to embrace certain aspects of the New Covenant. They've created a dysfunctional religious system that seems biblical, but is the very thing that Jesus warned us not to do.

In the following chapters of this book you will see much of what is new in the New Covenant that maybe you've overlooked. You may also discover some areas in your life where you've mixed in many Old Covenant practices.

When I look back on my own life as a Christian, I can now see where I attempted to mix the Old and New Covenants. That would explain why for several years my "religious system" seemed to be torn. God didn't "fix" my old religious system; He gave me a brand-new one.

As you read this book, it's my prayer that God would give you a new wineskin to hold His new wine.

TORN

CHAPTER 1

A New Covenant

I remember the day that I was given my first Bible. It was a maroon-colored Revised Standard Version, with my name printed in gold letters on the lower right side of the cover. Coming from a family of five kids, I remember being more impressed that I actually owned something with my name pre-printed on it than I was with the fact that I now had my very own Bible. Because I was raised in a church-going family, I knew that the Bible was an important book. But other than that, I had no real biblical knowledge nor any real desire to read it. That was pretty common among third grade boys in 1970.

Even though I had been in church almost every Sunday from the time I was born, I had never heard the message of salvation through faith in Jesus Christ. What I heard was: *Try really hard to be good so that maybe Jesus will let you into heaven.* It was the summer after my fourth grade year that I accepted Jesus as my Savior at a summer Bible camp. Not only did I receive a clear explanation of what it meant to be saved, but I was also encouraged to begin reading my still-like-new Bible.

What They Didn't Teach Me About the Bible

As a young Christian I was taught that the Bible contained the Old Testament, which was before Jesus, and the New Testament, which was after Jesus. While this is technically true, it leaves out some very important facts that make a very big difference when it comes to our understanding of God's plan for us today. More on that in a moment.

I was also taught that the Old Testament and the Old Covenant are the same thing, as well as the New Testament being synonymous with the New Covenant. This is not totally true. The Old Testament covers a period of approximately 4,000 years. The Old Covenant (also known as the Law or the Mosaic Covenant) covers the last 1,500 years of the Old Testament. That means that the Old Covenant covers only one-third of the time period recorded in the Old Testament. Granted, more writings in the Old Testament are connected to the Old Covenant, but the books of Genesis, Job, and over half of Exodus predate the Old Covenant.

I understand that all these numbers and all this history might seem boring to many of you, so let me just re-state things this way: The Old Covenant is *contained* in the Old Testament, but not all of the Old Testament *is* the Old Covenant. While that biblical truth may be new to many of you, get ready for what might be a real surprise.

You are not obligated to follow everything that is written in the Bible.

Some of you are nodding in agreement with this statement, some of you are wrinkling your forehead wondering if that is actually true, and a few of you may be wanting to close this book because of the heresy contained in it. I've actually had all three of these reactions at different times in my life, starting with the last one first.

After somehow getting through my teen years as an under-discipled Christian, I began to take my faith in Christ much more seriously as a young adult. The church I attended in my twenties and early thirties firmly grounded me in the truth that the Bible is God's inspired, living Word to man and our only source of truth for our faith in Jesus. I still strongly believe that today. I believe that the Bible, from Genesis to Revelation, is the inspired Word of God. I believe that we can learn something from every book of the Bible, in both the Old and New Testaments.

Because so many of us have correctly learned that the entire Bible is God's Word to us, it's hard for us to reconcile that with the fact that we're not obligated to follow all of the commands in the Bible, specifically many of those listed in the Old Covenant.

Again, just to be clear, I am *not* saying that the Old Testament is irrelevant to us today. The entire Old Testament gives us a rich picture of the character and nature of God, shows us the problem of sin, and points to our need for a Savior.

Covenants in the Old Testament

Before we go any further, it would be good to have a clear understanding of the word *covenant*. The dictionary simply defines it as "a usually formal, solemn, and binding agreement."[1] So, when we talk about the Old Covenant, we're actually talking about an old agreement. Likewise, the New Covenant is a new agreement. It should also be noted that covenants can either be bilateral or unilateral. A bilateral covenant is an agreement between two parties, each of whom would be responsible to carry out some sort of action. A unilateral covenant is more like a promise from one party to another. Someone who makes a unilateral covenant promises to carry out certain actions, regardless of any action by the other party. Both of these types of covenants are in the Bible.

You have probably already guessed by now that the Old

---

1   Merriam-Webster's Collegiate Dictionary (Eleventh Edition)

Covenant was not always referred to as "old." It didn't become the "old" covenant until the "new" covenant was instituted at the time of Jesus. Before the Old Covenant was old, it was most often referred to as *the Law*. People have also referred to it as the Mosaic Covenant, since God gave it through Moses.

You might be interested to know that the Old Covenant is not the only covenant in the Old Testament. In fact, there are three other prominent covenants made by God in the Old Testament. After the flood, God made a unilateral covenant with Noah that He would never bring another worldwide flood.[2] This is known as the Noahic Covenant. Approximately 500 years before the Mosaic Covenant, God made a unilateral covenant with Abraham in which He promised him that his descendants would become a great nation, and that all the world would be blessed through him.[3] This is known as the Abrahamic Covenant. God also made a covenant with King David that said his descendants would sit on the throne forever.[4] We know that Jesus is a descendant of David and will rule in eternity. This is known as the Davidic Covenant.

The Old Covenant (the Law) was a bilateral covenant between God and His chosen people, the nation of Israel. The centerpiece of the Old Covenant was the Ten Commandments, with many additional laws and religious regulations also in place. Since this was a bilateral covenant, the people had the responsibility of keeping these laws.

Now if you obey me fully and keep my covenant, then out of all nations you will be my treasured possession.
Exodus 19:5 NIV

---

2   Genesis 9:8-17
3   Genesis 12:2-3, 15:18-19
4   Psalm 89:3-4

If you've read much of the Old Testament at all, you know that the people didn't do a very good job of holding up their end of this bilateral covenant with God. Over the 1,500 years that the Old Covenant was in force, there were bright spots where godly kings and priests would lead by example and convince God's people to serve the Lord and to live righteously. However, much of that history is filled with generations of people who turned their backs on God and lived lives full of sin and shame.

One of the most important concepts in the Old Testament, and more specifically the Old Covenant, is that sin is a problem that must be dealt with. Another important truth that we can glean from the Old Testament is that giving people a list of written rules to follow is not a very effective way to keep them from falling into sin.[5] God knew this when He gave the Law through Moses, which is why He already had a plan in place to send the world a much-needed Savior along with a new covenant.

A New Covenant

We learn from reading the Old Testament that God's plan was for the Old Covenant to be temporary. About 600 years before the earthly ministry of Jesus and the New Covenant, and in the midst of the Old Covenant, God revealed His plan for a New Covenant through the prophet Jeremiah.

---

5   Romans 3:20

"The days are coming," declares the Lord,
"when I will make a new covenant
with the people of Israel
and with the people of Judah.
It will not be like the covenant
I made with their ancestors
when I took them by the hand
to lead them out of Egypt,
because they broke my covenant,
though I was a husband to them,"
declares the Lord.
"This is the covenant I will make with the people of Israel
after that time," declares the Lord.
"I will put my law in their minds
and write it on their hearts.
I will be their God,
and they will be my people.
No longer will they teach their neighbor,
or say to one another, 'Know the Lord,'
because they will all know me,
from the least of them to the greatest,"
declares the Lord.
"For I will forgive their wickedness
and will remember their sins no more."
Jeremiah 31:31-34 NIV

Six hundred years after God revealed His plan for the New Covenant through the prophet Jeremiah, Jesus announced the initiation of the New Covenant during an intimate dinner with His disciples.

In the same way, after the supper he took the cup, saying, "This cup is the new covenant in my blood, which is poured out for you."

Luke 22:20 NIV

Less than twenty-four hours later when Jesus died on the cross, the New Covenant was initiated, and what had been the current covenant (the Law) now became the Old Covenant. And not only did the Old Covenant become old, it became obsolete.

By calling this covenant "new," he has made the first one obsolete; and what is obsolete and outdated will soon disappear.
Hebrews 8:13 NIV

As I sit here today, I'm somewhat surprised by the number of Christians who adhere to many of the laws in the Old Covenant, even though the Bible clearly teaches that the Old Covenant is now obsolete. And yet, as I reflect on my own past, I now realize that I have also done the same thing. Like many other Christians, I embraced the truth of Jesus and His work on the cross. But instead of viewing that as the beginning of an entirely new agreement between God and man, I merely blended Jesus' New Covenant into the Old Covenant. My mixing of the old and new covenants was not purposeful, but more because of my ignorance of the clear delineation between the two covenants. That ignorance caused me many years of theological disharmony as I bumped back and forth between God's law and God's grace.

A Warning from Jesus

As Jesus was preparing the world for God's new agreement with man, He gave us a somewhat cryptic parable.

No one sews a patch of unshrunk cloth on an old garment, for the patch will pull away from the garment, making the tear worse. Neither do people pour new wine into old wineskins. If they do, the skins will burst; the wine will run out and the wineskins will be ruined. No, they pour new wine into new wineskins, and both are preserved.

Matthew 9:16-17 NIV

If you don't understand that Jesus was ushering in the kingdom of God here on earth along with His new covenant, then this parable will be very confusing. But given this new context, Jesus is basically telling us not to mix the old and new covenants. The Old Covenant stopped, and the New Covenant started. You don't mix the two. In this parable, the Old Covenant is represented by an old garment that has a hole in it. If you patch it with a new piece of material, the new material will shrink when washed and will actually tear the garment as it shrinks. *Torn.* Torn, because so many of us are trying to mix the new with the old. Jesus didn't come to patch up the Old Covenant, because a patch wouldn't fix it. It would actually make it worse. No, Jesus came with a brand-new garment for us.[6]

In this same parable, Jesus also uses the illustration of putting new wine into old wineskins. New wine continues to ferment and to give off gas for quite some time. An old wineskin has already been stretched as far as it will stretch, so when it's filled with new wine there's no stretch left for the expanding gases of the new wine. So, if you make the mistake of putting

---

6   Galatians 3:27

new wine into an old wineskin, it's going to tear and you're going to have a mess. *Torn.* Torn, because we're trying to mix the new with the old.

Those Foolish Galatians!

In the early days of the New Testament church, believers put their trust in Jesus and yielded to the leading of the Holy Spirit to guide and direct their lives. At that point Christianity was growing exponentially. But before long, some of those same Christians starting mixing the Old Covenant with the New Covenant. They professed Christ as their Savior, yet they reverted back to more of a works-oriented salvation and began to look back to the Old Covenant Law instead of looking to the Holy Spirit. Nowhere was this more prevalent than in the region of Galatia. This bothered the Apostle Paul so much that he addressed this situation in his letter to the Galatians.

Paul came right out and asked them, "You foolish Galatians! Who has bewitched you?"[7] He went on to acknowledge that they had started out as new believers by putting their faith in Jesus and walking with the Holy Spirit. But then he points out that they began to drift backward as they began to focus more and more on keeping the written Law from the Old Covenant as their source of righteousness, rather than trusting in Jesus and the leading of the Holy Spirit for their righteousness.

Although it seems somewhat ironic, probably the best summation of the New Covenant is given in the Old Covenant.[8] God states in Jeremiah 31:33 that instead of giving us rules and regulations written on stone (the Old Covenant), He would "write" His laws on our hearts. In other words, the Holy Spirit will lead and guide us in our thoughts and actions.

---

7   Galatians 3:1-3
8   Jeremiah 31:31-34

What's interesting to me is that the Old Covenant, with its set of written rules and regulations, was mostly a list of "do not." Do not kill. Do not lie. Do not steal. Do not have other gods. You get the picture. However, the New Covenant mostly speaks to what we should "do." Do give life. Do speak truth. Do be generous. Do love God. Again, I think you get the picture. Actually, the New Covenant holds us to a much higher standard than the Old Covenant. More on that in the next chapter.

The point is that living to a higher standard doesn't come from trying to follow a list of rules and regulations, but rather from following the leading of the Holy Spirit. When we put our trust in following a set of written rules, we're really putting trust (faith) in ourselves. That's because if we're finding our righteousness by following the Law, then we're going to have to follow it perfectly.[9] That's exactly what Paul was trying to tell the Galatians. What they had started in the power of the Holy Spirit they were now trying to complete by the power of their own flesh. Their patched-up religious system was torn and making a mess.

The Opposite of the Law

Over the past several years, I've heard many Christians contrast the Old Covenant law with the New Covenant message of grace. In many instances it has been referred to as "the law versus grace." I've heard many people speak of their church or pastor as one that preaches the message of grace instead of preaching the law. It's certainly true that we're no longer under the law, so there's no need to preach as if we were. And it's also true that the message of God's grace is a big part of the New Covenant. However, biblically speaking, the opposite of the law is not grace—it's faith.

9   Galatians 3:11-12

Clearly no one who relies on the law is justified before God, because "the righteous will live by faith." The law is not based on faith; on the contrary, it says, "The person who does these things will live by them."

Galatians 3:11-12 NIV

According to the Bible, you either live under the law or you live by faith. You can't live both. When you try to live under the law, you're basically saying that you don't trust what God said about the New Covenant. You don't trust the Holy Spirit to lead and guide you to live righteously. You have more faith in yourself to follow a written list of rules and regulations than you have faith in the Holy Spirit to speak to your heart and affect your actions. So, when it really comes down to it, Christians who are trying to live under the law have either been misled, or they're operating from a lack of faith.

Lots of New in the New Covenant

When Jesus instituted the New Covenant, He didn't introduce it as a series of small, incremental changes to the current religious system. No, what he initiated was an entirely new deal. And there's lots of *new* in this new agreement. You'd think that after 2,000 years, we as Christians would have a better understanding of all the *new* in the New Covenant. But after looking around it's apparent that many Christians, and even entire denominations, have yet to fully embrace much of the *new* in the New Covenant.

In the following chapters of this book, you will find what's new in the New Covenant. As you discover what's new, you'll also begin to see areas in your Christian life where perhaps you've been mixing the old with the new. Maybe, like me, you'll find that some of your old theology is torn. So, get your new wineskin ready, and let's start filling it with the new wine!

TORN

CHAPTER 2

A New Standard

Standard: \ˈstan-dərd\ *noun* something established by authority, custom,

or general consent as a model or example[10]

Uneasy

I've found that there's a quick test to determine whether or not you're a Christian who's mixing the Old Covenant in with the New Covenant. In order for you to take this test, I'm going to make a statement, and then I want you to examine how that statement makes you feel. I'm not asking what you *think* about the statement, but rather how it makes you *feel*. Ready? Here we go:

We are no longer under the Ten Commandments. There. Chew on that for a few seconds, and then decide how that statement makes you feel. If you have little or no reaction to this statement, then there's a good chance you're not mixing the Old with the New. However, if this statement makes you uneasy (or possibly even angry), then you definitely have one foot in the Old Covenant and one foot in the New.

If this statement causes you to feel uneasy, it's probably because you're thinking something along the lines that this gives people the notion that they can go out and do whatever they want. And you, being the good Bible-believing Christian

---

10   Merriam-Webster's Collegiate Dictionary

that you are, know that this can't possibly be true. And to your credit, you are correct. As Christians, we're not to go out and do whatever we want. So, in your mind, you're thinking, "See! That's why we need the Ten Commandments!" A few years ago, I was saying the same thing.

I spent years (many of them as a pastor) trying to ignore the seemingly contradictory ideas that we're no longer under the Law *and* that we're still to follow the Ten Commandments. But didn't Jesus refer to many of the Ten Commandments as the Law? Yes, He did. And doesn't Paul tell us over and over that we're no longer under the Law? Yes, he does. So, what's a guy to do? I mean, we can't just quit following the Ten Commandments, can we? That sounds like heresy! But then, while I was reading Jesus' words in the New Testament, a light bulb came on.

A New Understanding of an Old Truth

Sometimes we get a greater revelation of God's truth when we really dig deep into the Bible and uncover a small nugget of truth that adds to our understanding. But sometimes, and this was one of those times, we have to step back and take a wide look at God's Word to see concepts and principles that were right in front of our face the whole time. It's true that sometimes we can't see the forest because of all the trees. So, here's a huge truth that I discovered when I stepped back and looked at Jesus' teachings in the New Testament:

The New Covenant holds us to a much higher standard than the Old Covenant.

Yep. You read that right. The New Covenant demands much more of us as children of God than the Old Covenant could ever dream of. Before I go on to explain this further, I realize that I've just made a whole new group of people uneasy. If you're uneasy after what you just read, you're probably thinking that I've just thrown New Testament grace out the window and that I'm knocking on the door of works-based salvation. Nothing could be further from the truth. So just to put your mind at ease, I totally believe that we're saved by grace through faith in Jesus, and not by works.[11] I also believe in the finished work of the cross, and that our salvation comes through Jesus plus nothing. The high standards of the New Covenant are not a prerequisite for salvation, but rather a result of our salvation. There. Are we good now? Good. Let's move on.

Setting a New Standard

It's in Jesus' Sermon on the Mount where we begin to see Him place the bar much higher than it was in the Old Covenant. In several instances recorded in Matthew 5, Jesus would begin a sentence with the words, "You've heard it said...." He would then go on to quote a scripture verse from the Old Testament or to paraphrase a law from the Old Covenant. However, He didn't stop there. He would then continue with the words, "But I tell you...." It was at that point where He would announce a higher standard. Let's take a look at a few examples.

In Matthew 5:21 (NIV) Jesus says, "You have heard that it was said to the people long ago, 'You shall not murder, and anyone who murders will be subject to judgment.'" But in verse 22 He continues, "But I tell you that anyone who is angry with a brother or sister will be subject to judgment. Again, anyone who says to a brother or sister, 'Raca,' is answerable to the court. And anyone who says, 'You fool!' will be in danger of the fire of hell."

---

11   Ephesians 2:8-9

So as far as the Old Covenant is concerned, you're okay as long as you don't murder someone. Great! So far, so good! But then Jesus raises the bar by telling us that if we even call someone an idiot (*raca*), we've basically murdered them in our mind. If that's the case (and it is), then I've mentally murdered several dozen people who were driving too slow in the passing lane! I can live up to the standard of the Old Covenant as long as I don't physically kill the slow driver in the left-hand lane. But in order to live up to the standard of the New Covenant, I'm not even to call that same person an idiot, much less kill him. Holy Spirit, I'm going to need Your help on this! Could it be possible that Jesus is telling us that the New Covenant standard is to speak life and encouragement to the very people we're now mentally murdering?

In Matthew 5:27 (NIV) Jesus says, "You have heard that it was said, 'You shall not commit adultery.'" Okay... fair enough, Jesus. Then He goes on to add this in verse 28: "But I tell you that anyone who looks at a woman lustfully has already committed adultery with her in his heart."

I've been happily married to the same woman for over twenty-five years. We've actually been married for thirty-eight years. Well, you can do the math. Even through those tough years of marriage, I can honestly say that I never broke the Old Covenant commandment to not commit adultery. Yay for me! However, I cannot honestly say that I've never looked lustfully at another woman. I have. Back in the day, I would justify it by thinking that it was okay because I was not acting on it. I was wrong. God showed me many years ago how a lustful thought-life can negatively impact my relationship with my wife in many different ways. Had I continued to live in accordance with the Ten Commandments by simply not committing adultery in the physical sense, I'm not sure our marriage would have survived. It's only when I began to live up to the standard of the New Covenant that our marriage actually began to thrive. Could it be possible that Jesus is telling us that the New Covenant standard is better for marriages than the Old Covenant standard?

In Matthew 5:38 (NIV) Jesus said, "You have heard that it was said, 'Eye for eye, and tooth for tooth.'" In other words, under the Old Covenant, turnabout was fair play. If someone hurt you, it was completely acceptable to hurt them back. Continuing on in verses 39 and 40 Jesus says, "But I tell you, do not resist an evil person. If anyone slaps you on the right cheek, turn to them the other cheek also. And if anyone wants to sue you and take your shirt, hand over your coat as well."

As a pastor, I have counseled many people who have been hurt in one way or another by someone else. In most cases it took great restraint on the part of the person who was hurt not to lash back at the person who had hurt them. Some of the people were able to restrain themselves from retribution, but others were not. I can't remember any situation where retaliation made the situation better. Furthermore, most people who retaliated against those who had hurt them thought that vengeance would make them feel better. I have yet to talk to one person who could honestly say that their retribution actually made them feel better.

I think what Jesus is teaching here is clarified by Paul in Romans 12:19-20, when he basically says that our own wrath against someone who has hurt us can actually get in the way of God taking care of the situation Himself. Just as a point of clarification, Jesus is not telling us that we need to allow toxic and dangerous people into our lives. In fact, there are many biblical warnings against allowing those kinds of people into our lives. But not allowing a dangerous person access to our life and family is much different than retaliating against them.

Closely related to this is what Jesus taught in Matthew 5:43-44 (NIV). Jesus says, "You have heard that it was said, 'Love your neighbor and hate your enemy.' But I tell you, love your enemies and pray for those who persecute you."

When someone hurts us, our thoughts often turn toward retribution. But God's thoughts are always about redemption. In other words, God's goal is not always our goal. When we're hurting from someone else's action we want God to punish them, not help them. But if we allow the Holy Spirit to align our thoughts with God's thoughts, we could actually find ourselves praying for the same person who hurt us. Could it be possible that Jesus is telling us that the New Covenant standard is a better way to handle those who have hurt us than the Old Covenant standard?

One more. The ninth commandment says, "Do not lie." So, under the Old Covenant as long as we didn't lie, we were good. But in the New Testament Paul says in Ephesians 4:15 that we are to speak the truth in love. Please note the "in love" part. So not only are we not to lie, we're to speak the truth. And not only are we to speak the truth, we're to speak it in love.

I've learned from personal experience that if someone has a problem with lying, it's not very helpful to simply tell them to quit lying. It sounds reasonable, but it's not helpful. What's helpful is to encourage them to be speakers of the truth. I know it sounds like we're splitting hairs, but you don't stop lying by not lying. You stop lying by speaking the truth. Could it be possible that the New Covenant standard of speaking the truth in love is an upgrade from the Old Covenant commandment that says do not lie?

Could it be possible that that the New Covenant actually holds us to a higher standard than the Old Covenant? It seems to me that it's not only possible, but plainly obvious. I think I'm starting to see the forest through all those trees!

An Inside Job

Jesus didn't mince any words as He addressed the self-righteous Pharisees and teachers of the Law. They prided themselves on their careful attention to the Law, and they tried hard to gain a reputation as men who were faultless before God. While they focused on their outward actions, Jesus addressed their inward motivation. He compared them to a cup that was clean on the outside but filthy on the inside.[12] He was making the point that having a cup that is clean on the inside is much more important than having a cup that is sparkling clean on the outside, yet disgustingly dirty on the inside. And if that weren't enough, He goes on to compare them to whitewashed tombs which are brilliantly white and clean on the outside where everyone can see, but on the inside where no one can see, it's full of rottenness and darkness.[13] In most cases, the Pharisees and teachers of the Law were living up to the standard of the Old Covenant. In fact, they were so good at obeying the Old Covenant commandments that they started making up their own laws. Now they could appear even more righteous than ever before!

But Jesus wasn't fooled. He saw what was in their hearts. He saw how they treated others with disdain. He saw their greed. He saw their hypocrisy. While they could brag about their adherence to the Law, they certainly couldn't brag about their love for other people. And that's where Jesus was going with them. There's a new standard, boys. A higher standard. A New Covenant. A new way of thinking and doing things that won't fit into your current religious system.

---

12   Matthew 23:25-26
13   Matthew 23:27-28

Living Up to the New Standard

So, this begs the question: If people had a hard time living up to the standard of the Old Covenant, how in the world can we ever live up to the higher standard of the New Covenant? Well, thanks for asking.

The key to living up to the higher standard of the New Covenant was touched on in the previous chapter. In case you missed it, God spoke through the prophet Jeremiah and announced his plan for the New Covenant that wouldn't actually be instituted for another 600 years. In Jeremiah 31, God says that instead of us following rules that were written on stone, we would follow what the Holy Spirit writes on our hearts.[14] Instead of reading a list of rules and trying to follow them in our outward actions, we would now be guided and directed inwardly by the Spirit of Christ. In Paul's letter to the Galatians, he exhorted them to quit trying to follow the rules and regulations of the written Law and to fully yield to the Holy Spirit, who is the only one who can actually change our appetite for sin.[15] But here's where a problem begins to creep into the New Testament church.

When it comes right down to it, far too many pastors and church leaders, both past and present, don't really trust the Holy Spirit to keep believers from sinning. For some reason, these pastors and leaders feel much better about giving their congregation a list of do's and don'ts rather than teaching and encouraging them to walk with the Holy Spirit. Remember, Paul said if we walk in the Spirit, we won't gratify the desires of the flesh. In other words, if we tune into the Holy Spirit, pay attention to Him, and actually follow Him, we won't be sinning. But again, many pastors and leaders don't feel like they're doing their job unless they lay down the Law and then follow up with a heap

14   Jeremiah 31:33
15   Galatians 5:16-18

of guilt, shame, and condemnation for those who fall short. In essence, they're trying to play the role of the Holy Spirit because in reality, they don't trust the Holy Spirit to keep people on the straight and narrow. And by the way, this isn't limited to pastors and church leaders. Unfortunately, many church-goers who aren't in any type of leadership position have also adopted this behavior. Besides being unbiblical, it totally misrepresents the Holy Spirit and leaves those who are seeking God with a bad taste in their mouth. Our job is to speak the truth in love and let the Holy Spirit take it from there.

Because the New Covenant is a much higher standard, and because we as humans have had a hard time even living up to the lower standard of the Old Covenant, we're going to need some help. A lot of help. That's why the Father sent the Holy Spirit, also known as the Spirit of Christ.[16] God the Holy Spirit, the third part of the Trinity, empowers us from the inside out to live a life that is pleasing to the Father. There's no way we can live up to the high standard of the New Covenant without the work of the Holy Spirit in our lives. Closely following the Old Covenant Law will not even get us close to fulfilling what Jesus has asked us to do under the New Covenant. The Law is mostly made up of "don'ts," while the New Covenant is mostly made up of "do's." If we're going to do the "do's," we're going to need the power of the Holy Spirit at work in our everyday lives.

A New Command

I don't want to give you the idea that the Old Covenant, with all its rules and regulations, was bad. It wasn't bad. It just wasn't nearly as good as what the New Covenant is. The book of Hebrews extensively compares the Old Covenant with the New Covenant and refers to the latter many times as "better."

16   Romans 8:9

As you read on in this book, you'll see many quotations from the book of Hebrews and how the New Covenant is much more superior to the Old Covenant. But again, that's not to say that the Old Covenant was bad. If fact, in many of Paul's writings, he points out the good points of the Law and why it's an important part of our Christian history.

Even though there are mostly "don'ts" in the Law, they were there to show us how to treat God and other people in the right way. The Ten Commandments are really all about relationships. Our relationship with God, and our relationship with our parents, our neighbors, and even ourselves. So, it's no surprise, then, that God summed up the Old Covenant Law by telling us to love God[17] and to love our neighbor as ourselves.[18]

In Matthew 22:36-39 (NIV), Jesus was asked what the greatest commandment in the Law was. Instead of picking from the many "don'ts" in the Law, Jesus quoted from the Old Testament, "'Love the Lord your God with all your heart and with all your soul and with all your mind.' This is the first and greatest commandment. And the second is like it: 'Love your neighbor as yourself.'"[19]

Like many Christians, I have quoted the "love your neighbor as yourself" scripture many times as a New Covenant scripture because, well, it's in the New Testament, right? Yes, it's written in the New Testament, but if you'll go back and read it more closely, you'll see that the question Jesus is asked is in regard to the Old Covenant Law. So, Jesus answered the question exactly how it was asked. Love God and love your neighbor as yourself. Sounds pretty good, doesn't it? That's because it *is* good! But—and this is a big but—it's not the standard of the New Covenant. The standard in the New Covenant is much higher.

---

17   Deuteronomy 6:5
18   Leviticus 19:18
19   Matthew 22:37-39

I've read the New Testament many times in my life, and for some reason I've always read Jesus' words in John 13:34 as the same as the words in Matthew 22:39. I think it's because from a young age I was taught to memorize "Love your neighbor as yourself." Those are good words to memorize, but the problem is that those aren't the words in John 13:34 (NIV). In that verse, Jesus *doesn't* say to love your neighbor as yourself. Here's what He said. "A new command I give you: Love one another. As I have loved you, so you must love one another."

Boom. There it is. Clear as a bell. Do you see it? Instead of loving our neighbor as ourselves, we're now to love our neighbor as Jesus loves us. That's a huge difference! My love for myself is imperfect, inconsistent, and at times even selfish. But Christ's love for me is perfect, consistent, and sacrificial. Wow! Just think of Christ's love for you! Now think of you loving other people in that same way. Gulp! I don't think I've done all that great of a job loving others in the same way I love myself. And now Jesus wants me to up my game even more? God help me!

In all reality, God does help me. He has to. I can't even begin to attempt this level of love on my own. That's where the Holy Spirit comes in. Not only is the Holy Spirit there to lead and guide me so that I won't sin, He also is there to empower me to love others in the same way that Jesus loves me. In every aspect of life I need to always be asking, "Holy Spirit, what does love require of me in this situation?" If we ask with the right heart and right motivation, God is always more than willing to answer.

This New Covenant principle of loving others in the same way that Jesus loves us is not complicated, but it's far from being easy. It's not easy because love, as it's used here, is a verb—an action word. It's not necessarily a feeling. It means that we might have to do stuff. Even stuff we don't want to do. And, like you, I've already got enough stuff to do. But as I yield to the Holy Spirit's guidance and direction in my life, He will help me set my priorities straight so that Jesus' new command to love others like He loves me will not get pushed aside.

One thing I've learned over the years is that you can't give away what you don't have. In order for you to love others in the same way that Christ loves you, you need to know in your "knower" how much God loves you. Even the most marginal Christian would say, when asked, that God loves them. But those words often come from our heads and not our hearts. Until you get a revelation of God's great love for you—deep in your heart, where you can *feel* it and not just know it—you'll never be able to fully love others as Jesus has commanded. I can tell you until I'm blue in the face that God loves you, but I can never put it in your heart so you can feel it. Only the Holy Spirit can do that. Romans 5:5 says that it's the Holy Spirit who pours God's love into your heart. I can pour it into your head, but only the Holy Spirit can pour it into your heart. I know we're called believers and not feelers, and I know that feelings can be deceptive. However, God really wants you to feel His love for you in a very personal way. So, ask the Holy Spirit right now to pour the Father's love into you and to give you a fresh, new revelation of His great love for you. As He fills you with His love, you'll hardly be able to contain yourself, and you'll be looking for ways to love others in the same way that Jesus loves you. Oh, by the way, please don't contain yourself!

Imagine with me for a moment. What if millions of Christians all over the world began to live up to the higher standard of the New Covenant? What if we quit focusing on the "don'ts" and started focusing on the "do's"? What if we yielded fully to the Holy Spirit and let Him guide and direct us every day? What if we began to love others in the same way that Jesus loves us? As grandiose as this seems, this is not a pipe-dream. This is God's plan for His people under the New Covenant.

Are you ready to fully embrace God's upgrade? If so, keep reading.

TORN

CHAPTER 3

A New Church

I grew up in a mainline liturgical church that we attended every Sunday. There was no children's church option back then, so I learned to sit still and be quiet. If I was too fidgety or whiny, my mom would nudge my dad (actually, more like wake him up) and he would escort me outside for a little private lesson on behaving in church.

I remember having the sense that church was important, but I didn't know why. I heard about God and Jesus and heaven and hell. I caught just enough to know that I didn't want to go to hell, and apparently Jesus had something to do with that. So, in my young mind I began to think that the reason we went to church was so that Jesus wouldn't get mad and send us to hell. Finally, church made sense to me. It filled me with fear and anxiety, but it made sense. Unfortunately, what I thought made sense was actually nonsense, and I would go on into my early adult years before anyone challenged my way of thinking regarding the church and its purpose.

Why do you go to church? Or, maybe in your case, why do you *not* go to church? I'm sure you have your reasons, either way. But are your reasons valid? Just because something makes sense to you doesn't mean it's true. The fact is, Jesus has a plan for the New Testament Church, and it's important for us to come into alignment with His plan instead of us continuing in our wrong assumptions.

Jesus the Builder

**I will build my church, and all the powers of hell will
not conquer it.**
Matthew 16:18b NLT

The first time the word *church* is used in the Bible is when
Jesus said that He was starting to build it.[20] He wasn't talking
about a building, but rather a gathering of people. Our word
church comes from the Greek word *ekklesia*, which literally
means "a public assembly of people." Jesus used the very word
ekklesia to describe what He was building. Our English word
church and the Greek word *ekklesia* are closely related to the
Hebrew word *sunagoge*, which translates in English to *synagogue*, which also means a public assembly of people. I think
most of us have assumed that the word *synagogue* in the Bible
meant the building where the Jews met, but it doesn't really
mean that. It simply means a public gathering of people. It's
the same with our word *church*. We often refer to the building
as the church, when in reality it's not the building, it's the people that meet there.

One Saturday years ago, when our then four-year-old
granddaughter, Hannah, was staying with us, I stated that I
was going over to the church for a few minutes. Immediately
Hannah wanted to go with me, and so we jumped in the car
and drove to the church. With Hannah in tow, I unlocked the
door, turned on the lights, and walked into the empty sanctu-
ary. Hannah looked around for a few seconds, and then with a
confused look on her face asked, "Where's the church?" At four
years old, she had a better understanding of the church than
most adults I know.

Instead of using bricks and mortar to build His church,

---

20   Matthew 16:18

Jesus is using us as believers as building blocks, with Him as the cornerstone.

You are coming to Christ, who is the living cornerstone of God's temple. He was rejected by people, but he was chosen by God for great honor. And you are living stones that God is building into his spiritual temple.
1 Peter 2:4-5 NLT

Any reputable builder will tell you that the most important part of the construction project is to get your first corner of the building's foundation started correctly. Great care and time are taken to make sure that the first corner is at the right elevation, is square and level, and is oriented in the right direction. It's from the first corner that the rest of the structure grows and takes shape.

This same concept is critical in the church that Jesus is building. He is the Cornerstone, and every aspect of the church must reference back to Him. Unfortunately, over the years, certain man-made rituals and traditions that don't reference back to the Cornerstone have infiltrated many churches and denominations. While these rituals and traditions might not be evil, they can be a distraction from the real purpose Jesus has for His church.

Body Parts

While Peter uses the metaphor of building blocks for the believers who make up the church, Paul uses the metaphor of the human body.[21] The human body is made up of many parts, yet it is still one body. Each part of the body, though different,

---

21   1 Corinthians 12:12

has an important function, and the whole body is interdependent. It's the same in the church, and especially in the local church gatherings. Some people are hands, some are feet, some are ears, and so on. The only part of the body that you *can't* be is the head. That designation is reserved solely for Jesus.[22] Other than the head, you, as a believer in the kingdom of God, have a very important part to play in the body of Christ and the church that He is building.

This idea of every believer as an important, integral part of the church is vastly different from the religious structure of the Old Covenant and the workings of the temple and synagogues. Under the Old Covenant, the work of the ministry was to be carried out by an elite group of men who were born into a certain family line. It was their job as priests to minister to the needs of the people. There was a clear line of distinction between those who were ministered to and those who did the ministering. However, under the New Covenant, the work of the ministry is now to be carried out by every believer as they are trained and facilitated by church leaders who serve at the call of God.[23] Unfortunately, not everyone got the memo. Or perhaps they got the memo and just ignored it. In case you missed it, here's the memo:

Now these are the gifts Christ gave to the church: the apostles, the prophets, the evangelists, and the pastors and teachers. Their responsibility is to equip God's people to do his work and build up the church, the body of Christ.

Ephesians 4:11-12 NLT

---

22   Ephesians 1:22-23
23   Ephesians 4:11-12

Pastors vs. Ministers

For 2,000 years, pastors have played a prominent role in the New Testament Church, and rightly so. The problem is—and this is a big problem—many people, including many pastors, are confused about what the pastor of the local church should be doing. I must admit that in my first few years as a pastor, I, too, was not clear on my role. I just did what I saw most other pastors doing, which was to preach sermons on Sunday and be a spiritual ambulance the rest of the time. I, like most pastors, felt like it was my calling and duty to do all the work of the ministry because, well... I'm the pastor. How did I not see that this was totally unbiblical?

Eventually, I woke up to the truth of Ephesians 4:12 and became more of an equipper and facilitator of God's people. I still preach sermons and I still minister to other people, but my focus has shifted to that of an equipper.

Not everyone is called to be a pastor, but every believer is called to be a minister. In Ephesians 4:12 there are several different English words used that are translated from the Greek word *diakŏnia*, which means "to serve or to minister." I think it's unfortunate that in our society we've used the word *minister* to mean the same as *pastor*. They're not the same words. *Pastor* literally means "shepherd," and *minister* means "to serve others." Not everyone is called to shepherd a church, but everyone is called to serve others. But because of the way we've interchanged these two words for so long, most Christians don't see themselves as a minister, because they don't see themselves as a pastor.

About 400 years after the New Testament Church was launched, certain powerful church leaders began to mix many Old Covenant religious practices into the New Covenant church. One of those practices marked the return of the "priest" into the church. (In the next chapter we'll dive into the subject of the New Testament priesthood).

If you remember from our previous discussion, the priest in the Old Covenant was responsible to do the work of the ministry, and that's just what these New Testament "priests" began to do—all the work of the ministry. For the first 300 years the Christian church experienced exponential growth, largely due to the fact that the believers saw themselves as ministers and acted on it. But at some point, these few men thought of a "better" way. We can guess at their motives for doing this all day long, but the bottom line is that for the next 1,000 years, the "church" as most of the world knew it had reverted back to many of the obsolete religious structures from the Old Covenant.

Thankfully, in the late 1400s the Holy Spirit moved in a powerful way, and many godly men like Martin Luther began to courageously speak out against the errors of the prevailing church structure. In a relatively short time, the biblical role of the pastor was brought back into the church. However, it has been a long road to restore the mindset of all believers as ministers.

The Model Church

Ten days after the ascension of Jesus into heaven, the Holy Spirit came and filled the 120 believers in the Upper Room, and the church was born. The next day the church grew to 3,000, and after that it was off and running. It's the gospel writer Luke who gives a good picture of how the early church operated in Acts 2.[24] Many people, including myself, refer to this as the model church. It's not the perfect church, because it's made up of imperfect people; but it is a model for us to follow as a New Testament church.

As Luke begins his description of the model church in

---

24   Acts 2:42-47

Acts 2:42, he starts off by stating that the believers devoted themselves to learning. He doesn't say that they sometimes showed up and hoped for a good (but short) sermon. They actually *devoted* themselves to learning. *Devoted* is a strong word. We may think of devoting ourselves to our family, or possibly our career. But have you ever thought about devoting yourself to learning more about Jesus, His New Covenant, and the kingdom of God? Jesus used the term *discipleship*,[25] and that's exactly what the early church was engaged in and what should be a focus for us today.

Right after Luke talks about the importance of discipleship in the early church, he details the deep fellowship among the believers.[26] They shared meals together, prayed together, took communion together, and were there to help meet each other's needs. Over the years, I've heard more than a few people who self-identify as a Christian say that they don't have to go to church to be a Christian. While there is a small sliver of truth in that statement, they're missing the bigger point. Believers who aren't part of a good, local church are missing a huge component of the New Testament church, and that component is fellowship. Not a shallow, put-on-your-smiley-face kind of fellowship, but rather a deep fellowship where people take the time to invest in each other.

Also included in the description of the model church is the presence of miraculous signs and wonders.[27] I would venture to guess that most churchgoers today would be weirded-out if miraculous signs and wonders were to happen in their church. And yet, this is supposed to be the norm when believers gather together.[28]

For the first nine years of my pastorate, I didn't really see

---

25   Matthew 28:19
26   Acts 2:42
27   Acts 2:43
28   Mark 16:17-18

what you would call signs and wonders. We saw people get saved and baptized. We saw our church grow. And on rare occasions, someone might testify to some type of physical healing. As far as most people were concerned, we were a normal, healthy church that most people enjoyed attending. But after those first nine years, I began to experience a type of holy discontent. I was discontent because I knew the model for a New Testament church was to experience miraculous signs and wonders. Even Jesus said that miracles and healings would be the sign of His kingdom.[29] But I was nervous. What would the people think? Wouldn't it be kind of weird? What if things got out of control?

Actually, things *had* to get out of control. My control. God showed me that in my effort to keep things from getting "weird" in the church, I had in essence sterilized the church. He used that exact word with me. *Sterilized*. As I began to loosen my control and let God move in the way He wanted to, we began to see miraculous signs and wonders, mostly in the area of physical healing. Week after week there were testimonies of verified miraculous healings. Some, like a broken bone popping back into place in front of our very eyes, seemed downright weird! It was instances like these that helped me to see that there should be some weird things happening in a New Testament church. Not *bad* weird, but *good* weird. In the local church there should be some supernatural expression of God's power that causes people to smile and say, "Wow. That was kind of weird."

As Luke continues writing in Acts 2, he talks about the fact that believers gathered together every day (at a building) and worshiped God. Every day! And now we have Christians who want brownie points for attending church twice a month! Here's the unvarnished truth: God wants you in church.[30]

---

29   John 14:12, Matthew 10:8
30   Hebrews 10:25

Church attendance was of paramount importance in the model church of Acts 2.

Luke concludes his description of the early church by placing an importance on salvation.[31] After all, that was Jesus' main reason for coming to earth and dying on the cross. Our local churches must be a place where connecting lost people to Jesus is a priority. That's the kind of church Jesus is building.

God's Secret Weapon

God planned the New Testament church before the beginning of time, yet He kept much of it a secret until it was unveiled just after Jesus' ascension to heaven.[32] There are really two questions that come to mind regarding this.

First, what was the big secret?

The best-kept secret of the New Testament church is that *every* believer carries the power and presence of God through the Holy Spirit. Before the Day of Pentecost when the church was launched, the Holy Spirit was only given to certain people at certain times for a certain task. But now, the supernatural power of the Holy Spirit is available to every believer 24/7.

So that brings up a second question. Why did that have to be kept so secret?

Think about it. Satan wanted Jesus dead and gone from the earth, because the power that Jesus carried with Him thwarted the work of the devil. By the power of the Holy Spirit, Jesus was undoing the work of Satan.[33] It's no stretch to imagine that Satan was doing the "happy dance" the moment that Jesus died on the cross. Fast-forward fifty days to the Day of Pentecost. That's the day that the Holy Spirit came and filled all who were

---

31   Acts 2:47
32   Ephesians 3:9-11
33   Acts 10:38

Christ-followers. From that day forward, every time a person steps out and puts their faith in Jesus, they are filled with the supernatural power and presence of God the Holy Spirit. It's Satan's worst nightmare. Now, instead of one person roaming the earth with the power of the Holy Spirit, suddenly there are hundreds, then thousands, and then millions, and now millions and millions. If Satan would have known this, he would have done everything in his power to keep Jesus alive and to keep the Holy Spirit from coming and filling every believer.

But Satan cannot stop it, because Jesus is building His church, and the gates of hell will not prevail.[34]

The church that Jesus is building, the New Covenant church, isn't a namby-pamby, weak, boring, dried-out organization that struggles to survive. No, the church that Jesus is building is filled with His supernatural power and presence. It's a church where people are devoted to learning, in deep fellowship with one another, and committed to meeting together in praise and worship on a consistent basis. It's a church where people who are far from God are brought into His presence. It's a church that is God's not-so-secret weapon.

It's a church that Jesus wants you to be a part of.

---

34   Matthew 16:18

TORN

CHAPTER 4

A New Priesthood

In the mainline protestant denomination that I grew up in, we referred to the leader of our church as "pastor." When I got into elementary school, many of my classmates talked about having a "priest" as the leader of their church. When I was in first or second grade, I remember going home from school one day and asking my mom why we didn't have a priest in our church. Her answer was something to the effect of us not needing a priest, which created even more questions in my mind. Like most kids that age, I was inquisitive, but I also had a short attention span and was easily distracted. So even though I had these questions, I didn't seem to care that they weren't adequately answered in my young mind.

When I was ten years old, my aunt talked me into going to summer Bible Camp. It was there that I first heard the clear message of God's plan of salvation and responded to it with all the sincerity that a ten-year-old boy can muster. It was real. Even though I continued to attend church services every Sunday, Sunday school, and even confirmation classes, I wasn't discipled in a way that connected with me. So, even though I was saved and wanted to do the right thing, my high school years were a roller coaster ride of spiritual highs and fleshly lows.

During those low times, I would sometimes think that maybe becoming a Catholic priest would even out my spiritual roller coaster ride and force me to live a life of righteousness every day. At that point I had never even been to a Catholic mass. The only time I had seen a priest in action was at my great-grandfather's funeral. Being Protestant, I had also considered becoming a pastor, but becoming a priest just seemed like a more stringent path to force myself to live a holy life. I'm pretty sure I'm not the only one who's ever had these thoughts!

But then, a few things happened. First, I learned that a priest couldn't be married, and I was pretty sure I could never spend the rest of my life in celibacy. Then, I heard that I would have to go to four years of college and then three more years of seminary. Even though I had done well in high school, I could hardly bear the thought of seven more years of school. And then, there was that nagging question that still lingered in the back of my mind regarding the legitimacy of the priesthood in the New Testament Church.

Well, it turns out that I didn't become a priest. I did, however, become a pastor. It took me until age forty, but God finally got me there!

So, what about you? What are your thoughts regarding the legitimacy of the priesthood in Christianity? Some of you may have very strong beliefs one way or the other, but there's a good chance that many of you haven't really given it much thought. It's important, though, that we not only have a strong belief regarding the priesthood, but that our belief actually aligns with God's teaching in the Bible. A lack of biblical understanding regarding the role of priests in the New Covenant can cause believers to miss much of what God has for them in this life and can lead to a form of powerless Christianity.

Priests in the Old Testament

A *priest* is defined in the dictionary as one who performs rites and rituals to God on behalf of others. They're a go-between, a mediator between God and man. Even though many of the world's religions have priests as part of their religious systems, the idea originated with God the Father before the beginning of time. You don't have to read very far in the Bible before you begin to see priests appearing here and there. Our first introduction to a priest comes to us in Genesis 14, where we're introduced to a man named Melchizedek. He wasn't just an ordinary man, but also a king in addition to being a priest. More on him later. It's important to note, though, that the priestly ministry of Melchizedek came about 500 years before God instituted the Old Covenant priesthood through Aaron and the tribe of Levi.

Around 1,500 B.C. (give or take a hundred years), God gave Moses the Law and its associated priesthood. Under the Old Covenant, the priests came only from the Jewish tribe of Levi and began their priestly ministry at age thirty. It was their responsibility to carry out the daily animal sacrifices and to act as a mediator between God and man. It was also their duty to see that all the rites and rituals of the Law were carried out as prescribed by God. They were led by the high priest, who was the only one who had access to the Most Holy Place—the dwelling place of God Himself. Once a year, the high priest would enter the Most Holy Place and offer the blood of an innocent animal to atone for the sins that God's people had committed during the year. All of this was to point to the perfect sacrifice that was to come.

Because Jesus was the perfect sacrifice, no further blood sacrifice is needed under the New Covenant. Furthermore, the death of Jesus gave all believers immediate and full access to the Most Holy Place—the dwelling place of God—which is no longer housed in a building built by man. Now God's dwelling place is not only *among* His people, but *in* His people.

Therefore, there is now no need for a priest to make sacrifices for us. Nor is there a need for a priest to speak to God on our behalf. It probably wasn't easy for an Old Covenant priest to hear that much of his job was no longer necessary, and that the rest of his job could now be done by uneducated men and women. Women? Seriously? And Gentiles, too? You've got to be kidding me!

That had to hurt.

So, what was an Old Covenant priest to do? And what about all the people that used to come to him to have their sins forgiven and to have him speak to God for them?

Priests in the New Testament?

Just like 2,000 years ago, we can either decide to fully embrace the New Covenant with all its changes, or we can try to mix a little of the Old Covenant in to make our own religious concoction. The problem is that many Christians, and even entire denominations, have done this—much to their peril. Remember, Jesus warned that if we try mixing the Old and New Covenants, something is going to tear. And it's going to make a mess.

So, are there priests in the New Covenant, or not? The answer is clearly yes. But the priesthood in the New Testament is much different than the priesthood under the Law. The rest of this chapter is devoted to revealing biblical truth as it pertains to priests in the New Testament.

Welcome to the Holy and Royal Priesthood

In 1 Peter 2:5, Peter comes right out and tells us that all true believers in Jesus are priests. Not Old Covenant priests, but New Covenant priests. He even attaches the word "holy" to describe our priesthood. The most basic definition of the word *holy* as it's used here is "separated for use by God." In other words, we're called to separate ourselves from the sinful, self-centered acts of the world and offer our lives to be used for God's purpose.

There are groups of people all over the world who, in the name of God, live a secluded life dedicated to prayer and study, and who are widely regarded as "holy." But technically speaking, you can't live a secluded life and be holy both at the same time. It's true that the first part of the definition of holiness is separation, but it doesn't end there. The last part of the definition of holiness is "to be used by God." God is in the people business, and as we'll see later in this chapter, God uses *us* to minister to other people. So, unless we're around unholy people, we can't really fulfill our duties as New Covenant priests. Warren Wiersbe once wrote that when it comes to holiness, separation is not isolation—it's contact without contamination. That's a great way to view our human interaction as a holy priest.

Not only does Peter say that we're holy priests, he goes on to say in 1 Peter 2:9 that we're also *royal* priests. Because the attribute of humility is so clearly taught by Jesus, many Christians struggle with being identified as royalty. But that's what you are! If your Father is the King, then that makes you royalty! As royalty, we can (and should) act with humility, but we should also act in a royal manner. What does it mean to act as royalty?

In the days of kings and kingdoms, a king would send forth men from his royal court to carry out his decrees. As they rode up on their horses, they would announce that they were coming in the name of the king. That meant that they were operating with all the power and authority of the king. It's the same for us as believers. As royal priests, we come in the name of King Jesus, with all the power and authority He has given us. We are called to carry out the desires of the King and to advance His kingdom here on earth. Even though we are royal priests, we don't get to call the shots. We have a High Priest, and His name is Jesus.[35] So, as God's priests today, we must work together at the direction of our Great High Priest.

It's interesting to note that the Old Covenant priests were required to come from the tribe of Levi, but Jesus was from the tribe of Judah. This is one of several indications that the New Covenant is different than the Old Covenant.

It's also interesting to note that our High Priest is always praying for us.[36] Under the Old Covenant, the priests would offer prayers to God on behalf of the people. Under the New Covenant, we still have a Priest offering prayers to God on our behalf, but the big difference is that this Priest is Jesus Christ himself.

Our Priestly Sacrifices

We've established the fact that there is a New Covenant priesthood, and that all true believers are priests, with Jesus as our High Priest. But are you aware that in addition to being a priest, you are called to make priestly sacrifices?

You also, like living stones, are being built into a spiritual house to be a holy priesthood, *offering spiritual sacrifices* acceptable to God through Jesus Christ.
1 Peter 2:5 NIV

Under the Old Covenant, priests would offer many types of sacrifices on behalf of God's people. Most of these were animal sacrifices that were made to cover the sins of the peo-

---

35   Hebrews 7:28
36   Hebrews 7:24-25

ple. These sacrifices did not take sin away, but merely covered it until Jesus came to make the perfect sacrifice. Because the Bible tells us that Jesus' perfect sacrifice put an end to the need of any further blood sacrifices, many New Testament believers think that there's now no need for any more sacrifices. It is true that there's no more need for future blood sacrifices, but that doesn't mean there aren't sacrifices under the New Covenant. There are. These sacrifices are to be made by us, as holy and royal priests, as we carry out the desires of our High Priest and King. It's very important to understand that these New Covenant sacrifices are not a prerequisite for our salvation. They are an evidence of our salvation.

A Living Sacrifice

In Romans 12:1, Paul tells us that we are to offer our lives as a *living* sacrifice to God. Jesus didn't ask us to die for Him, although most of us would. He asks us to live for Him. That doesn't mean that everyone should quit their jobs and become a pastor or a missionary, but it does mean that we should glorify Him as we live our everyday lives. But what does that look like?

> **You are royal priests, a holy nation, God's very own possession. As a result, you can *show others the goodness of God*, for he called you out of the darkness into his wonderful light.**
> **1 Peter 2:9 NLT**

There it is in black and white. As holy and royal priests of God, we're to show the world His goodness.

As strange as it may sound, many people (even many

Christians) struggle with accepting the fact that God is good. All the time. It's one thing to tell people about the goodness of God, but it's quite another to *show* them the goodness of God. When people look at your life, would they see that God is good? It doesn't mean that you never have any problems, and that things always seem to go your way. It means that in the midst of the trials and tribulations that come from living life, you maintain an attitude of peace, hope, and joy. These attributes are extremely attractive, yet very elusive, to those who are watching your life. If they know that you're a Christian, they're hoping to see something different from what the world has to offer. Are you showing the goodness of God to them?

As New Testament priests, we're called to be ambassadors for Christ and to work to reconcile people back to God.[37] The most effective way to do this is for people to see the goodness of God at work in our own lives. It doesn't matter what your job is, or even whether or not you have a job. It doesn't matter what your economic status is, or your level of education. Wherever you are, you can live your everyday life as a sacrifice to God by showing those around you His goodness.

But you can't show the goodness of God to others if you don't first allow Him to work in your own life. The people around you might appreciate your good deeds, but what they're really drawn to is the fruit of the Holy Spirit that is shown in your life. In Galatians 5:22-23, Paul lists the fruit of the Spirit as love, joy, peace, patience, kindness, goodness, faithfulness, gentleness, and self-control. These aren't separate fruits (plural)—these are all one fruit. In other words, if you're truly letting the Holy Spirit lead and guide you, you will see all nine of these attributes in your life. This fruit is nothing that you can produce on your own. It only comes into your life as you yield to the leading of the Holy Spirit. I often tell those I speak to that if they truly walk in the Holy Spirit, fruit happens.

---

37   2 Corinthians 5:20

I've said this so many times in my preaching that one of the members in my church had a bumper sticker custom-made for me that simply says, "Fruit Happens." When fruit happens in your life, people will notice, and God's goodness will be shown to them.

In order for this to happen, you're going to have to make some sacrifices. You're going to have to sacrifice your desire to follow your flesh instead of the Holy Spirit. You're going to have to sacrifice whining and complaining. You're going to have to sacrifice your urge to gossip. You're going to have to sacrifice your self-centeredness, your anger, your fear. You may even have to sacrifice some of your busyness. No one ever said that New Covenant sacrifices are easy.

A Sacrifice of Praise

Therefore, let us offer through Jesus a continual *sacrifice of praise* to God,

proclaiming our allegiance to his name.

Hebrews 13:15 NLT

The Bible tells us to offer a sacrifice of praise to God. I think most Christians are aware that we are to give God praise and worship, but the idea of praise as a sacrifice might be a new concept to many.

Over the years, I have grown in my connection with God through praise and worship. In my early years as a church attender, I didn't have a clear understanding of worship, whether inside or outside the context of the Sunday morning church service. For many of those years I viewed the songs that we sang together on Sunday morning as more of a warm-up for the sermon. I didn't really grasp the idea that this was a time set aside to enter into the presence of God and give Him our heartfelt thanks and adoration. Now that I have a better understanding of praise and worship, I enjoy coming into the presence of God and giving Him my praise.

That being said, I can't honestly say that I am always excited to enter into a time of praise and worship to God. There are times when my thoughts get bogged down in the things of this world, and worry and anxiety begin to press in. These are the times when praising God seems difficult, and yet these are the times when worshiping God can be just what we need the most. Worshiping God in the midst of a storm can be one of the most liberating and life-changing things we can do.

I'm not proud to admit this, but in the past when I didn't *feel* like worshiping God, I would purposefully not praise Him because I didn't want to be a hypocrite. I felt it was hypocritical to offer praise to God when I didn't *feel* like doing it. But then I realized a couple of things that changed my mind.

First, I remembered that we're called "believers," and not "feelers." I know that God wants us to feel what we believe, but we can't base our beliefs off of our feelings. I realized that it's not hypocritical to show love to my wife even if I don't *feel* particularly loving at that moment. Along with that, I realized that love is not just a feeling, but an action. I'm pretty sure Jesus didn't *feel* like dying on the cross for us, but He did it because of His great love for us. That doesn't make Jesus a hypocrite. In fact, it reveals Him as the most loving person in the universe.

Secondly, I read Hebrews 13:15, where it tells us to offer a *sacrifice* of praise. Not everyone who offers a sacrifice feels like doing it. Again, Jesus is our example here. He didn't *feel* like sacrificing His life for us,[38] but He did. If Jesus can offer such a great sacrifice for me, I can surely offer a sacrifice of praise to Him.

---

38   Matthew 26:39

A Sacrifice of Works

For centuries, certain elements of the church propagated the myth that we are saved by our good works. Thanks to people like Martin Luther, we now understand that we are saved by God's grace when we put our trust in Jesus.[39] But because of our history of bad teaching regarding good works as a way to salvation, we've tended to "throw the baby out with the bath water." While most Christians have gladly embraced the truth of salvation by grace through faith, many have also ignored the biblical truth that we are called to do good works. As a holy and royal priest, you are called to do good works for others and to share with those in need.

And don't forget to *do good* and to *share* with those in need.
These are the sacrifices that please God.
Hebrews 13:16 NLT

Helping others in their time of need is rarely convenient for us. That's why it's called a sacrifice. To truly help others, you will need to sacrifice your time and even some of your possessions, including money. This cuts right to the heart of our self-centered lives. My wife and I have always had a strong desire to help people; but to be honest, that desire has not always turned into action. As we have grown in our faith, we have done a better job of turning our desire to help people into action. We're still a work in progress, but I think we're doing a much better job than we have done in the past.

One of the things that used to hinder my actions in helping others was the concern that some people might end up taking advantage of me. It wasn't an unfounded concern, because I had

39   Ephesians 2:8-9

seen people take advantage of those who tried to help them. I myself had been in several situations where it appeared people were taking advantage of my generosity. But several years ago, the Holy Spirit revealed to me that if I was never willing to be taken advantage of, I could never fully minister to people. I understand that our generosity can enable certain people to continue in their dysfunction, and we don't want that. In those cases, we need discernment from the Holy Spirit and perhaps a dose of tough love. That being said, we don't want to dwell on all the ways someone might take advantage of us if we help them. Otherwise, we'll never step out and help anyone. As holy and royal priests to God, we're clearly called to help others by sharing our time and our treasure.

As we bring this chapter to a close, I want to make one thing abundantly clear: Our sacrifices to God as New Covenant priests don't appease Him, they please Him.[40] The last thing we want to do is put ourselves under a legalistic yoke of bondage, where we think we need to work hard to satisfy the wrath of God. God's wrath has already been satisfied by the blood of Jesus.

So, remember as you carry out your priestly call under the New Covenant that you're not doing it to satisfy a demanding taskmaster; you're doing it to please your loving Father.

---

40   Hebrews 13:16

TORN

CHAPTER 5

A New Temple

The temple played a very important role in the Old Covenant. It was one structure that consisted of three distinct areas. The outer court was a meeting place for God's people and was accessible to everyone. The Holy Place was where the priests offered prayers and sacrifices, and only the priests themselves were allowed to enter. The Most Holy Place, also known as the Holy of Holies, was where the ark of the covenant was located, and most notably was the symbolic dwelling place of God. Access was limited to the High Priest, and only once per year on the Day of Atonement. The Bible tells us of a time in the temple when the presence of God was so glorious and so real that the priests couldn't even carry out their priestly duties.[41] All they could do was fall on the floor in praise and worship. So, as you can see, the Old Covenant temple was really the epicenter of God's work among His people.

Seven weeks after Jesus' death and resurrection, God's temple was relocated. On the Day of Pentecost, 120 followers of Jesus were praying together when suddenly, a mighty wind began blowing (inside the room, mind you) and tongues of fire appeared above the head of every person in the room.[42] If you think about it for a minute, God had previously shown His presence in the form of fire. God first appeared to Moses as a burning bush. Shortly after that, God led His people through the desert as a cloud during the day and as a pillar of fire at

41   1 Kings 8:10-11
42   Acts 2:1-4

night. Now, on the Day of Pentecost, that one pillar of fire became many small pillars of fire above every believer's head. God was giving us a clear illustration that His presence had now taken up residence in every believer.

It shouldn't have been a big surprise to Jesus' followers, because He had told them it was going to happen. Okay, maybe He didn't say exactly *how* it would happen, but He did say it would happen. He told them that the Holy Spirit, who had lived among them in the person of Jesus, would soon come to live *in* them.[43] And fifty days after Jesus' death, that's exactly what happened. The dwelling place of God had been relocated.

Don't You Realize?

After nearly a thousand years of going to the temple as the dwelling place of God, it's understandable that many New Covenant believers at that time had difficulty grasping the idea that *they* were now the dwelling place of God. In fact, even former pagans struggled with this concept. Even though pagans had never set foot in the Old Testament temple, they did, however, have temples of their own. Almost every religion on the face of the earth believes that their deity dwells in a specific location, with that certain place being very sacred to them. So, whether they were Jewish followers of Christ or converted pagans, many seemed to struggle with the truth that they housed the very presence of God. Most non-Christian religious people don't have a problem viewing the physical dwelling place of their god as a sacred, holy place. But it seems to me that many Christians struggle with the fact that their body is the holy dwelling place of God Almighty.

One Sunday morning not too long ago, the members of the church that I pastor walked into our church building to

---

43   John 14:17

find garbage strewn everywhere. Pizza boxes, empty soda cans, empty milk cartons, crumpled paper, and all kinds of trash were scattered all over. As people walked into the worship service that morning, most had a look of horrid surprise. Garbage is not something you expect to see when you walk into a Sunday morning service. You might be thinking that we were the target of vandalism the night before. But that wasn't the case. *I* did it.

I expected that people would be bothered by all the trash in our place of worship. And they were. At least, at first. But it wasn't long before most of them knew that I was up to something. Apparently, I have a hard time keeping a straight face. And most of you are probably way ahead of me on where I'm going with this illustration.

As we gathered that Sunday morning, I asked folks how all the garbage in the church building made them feel. While most of them eventually figured that it was all leading to some sort of sermon illustration, their first reaction was generally one of objection and disgust. And rightfully so. It's not honoring to God to treat our place of worship in such a way.

But then came my next question:

"So why is it okay for your life to be like this?"

That was one of the hardest questions I've ever asked my congregation. It was hard because I'm not a legalistic person, and I could see how this question could be taken from a very legalistic standpoint. I'm also not the kind of pastor who routinely gut-punches his people; however, I did want to make the same point that Paul made in 1 Corinthians 6:19:

Don't you realize that your body is the temple of the Holy Spirit, who lives in you and was given to you by God?[44]

---

44   New Living Translation

It's easy for Christians to walk into a physical structure that is often referred to as "God's House" and notice if there's garbage lying all around. And not only do they notice, they object to it and want to do something about it. But what about our own lives? If we're really God's House—and we are—shouldn't we at least be equally offended at the garbage that we allow to linger in our lives? Garbage in our life comes in many forms—gossip, anger, greed, worry, fear, pornography, sexual immorality, lust, addictions, laziness, self-righteousness, hypocrisy, apathy, and self-centeredness, just to name a few.

In case you feel like I'm on my high horse pointing my finger at you, I want you to know that God's been dealing with me on some of these same issues, especially regarding my physical health. I've always been reasonably healthy, despite my love of junk food and my disdain for physical exercise. But as I get older, I realize that I'm letting God's temple fall into disrepair. If my body is God's temple—and it is—then I need to be a good steward of it and take care of what He's entrusted to me. It also means that I need to keep out the garbage of gossip, self-righteousness, hypocrisy, unforgiveness, pride, and all the other garbage previously listed.

House Rules

The Bible tells us that our body is a temple, but it's not *our* temple. The temple belongs to God. Right after Paul writes that we are the temple of God, he goes on to say this in 1 Corinthians 6:19-20:

> **You do not belong to yourself, for God bought you with a high price. So you must honor God with your body.**[45]

---

45   New Living Translation

Here's a question for you: Do you consider it a privilege to house the presence of God? Maybe you've never thought about it. It's one thing to know the fact that as believers we house the presence of God, but it's another thing to consider it as a privilege. To be honest, I hadn't really thought about it that way until recently. I had known that I am God's temple as a fact but didn't even stop to think about it as a privilege. That's important to know, because when we understand that we've been given a great privilege, we honor that privilege and the One who gave it to us. The fact that we're to keep the garbage out of our lives is not a matter of religious legalism, it's a matter of honor.

Most households have some form of house rules. Some may include rules such as no shoes on the carpet, no pets on the couch, clear your dishes from the table, and so on. Other house rules may be more attitudinal, such as no disrespectful talk or profanity. At any rate, house rules are set up to keep some semblance of order and cleanliness. But did you know that God has house rules for His New Covenant temple? There are only two, and they're not complicated. I'm not saying they're easy to follow; I'm just saying they're easy to understand.

God's House Rule #1: Do not grieve the Holy Spirit.[46]

The word *grieve* as it's used here is a verb, and it means to cause sorrow. So how do we cause the Holy Spirit to experience sorrow? We grieve the Holy Spirit when we disagree with Him. You might be trying to think whether you've ever disagreed with the Holy Spirit—but let me assure you, you have. Most of us would not want to knowingly or willfully disagree with God, but we do it more often than we might imagine.

There's actually a word in the Bible for disagreement with

---

46   Ephesians 4:30

God. It's called *sin*. When we think of sin, we tend to think of the "biggies," like murder, stealing, adultery, lying, etc. But the word *sin* literally means to miss the mark. Certainly, we miss the mark if we murder someone or commit adultery or steal or lie. But God's Word also says that we miss the mark when we do such things as complain, gossip, sow discord, and walk in unforgiveness. God clearly tells us in His Word not to do these things. So, if we end up doing them, we're in essence disagreeing with God. Whenever we continue in our disagreement with God, we grieve the Holy Spirit.

I'm well aware that even though we're followers of Christ, from time to time we will miss the mark. I'm also well aware that God has already forgiven us, and all He's asking from us is that we agree with Him that we have sinned.[47] I don't think we cause undue grief to God when we're quick to recognize our sin and quick to turn from it. It's our willful continuance in that sin that causes the Holy Spirit to grieve.

It's important to know that grieving the Holy Spirit is not the same as angering Him. God's anger toward your sin was satisfied by the death of Jesus on the cross. He's not mad at you now, nor will He ever be. Jesus took care of that. That's not to say, however, that your sin doesn't cause God to feel sorrow. Because it does. This isn't meant to make you feel guilt-ridden and full of shame—that's from the devil. It's simply to remind you that the choices you make in your personal life that go against God's Word affect more than just you. Those actions pull on the heartstrings of God Himself because of His great love for you. When my two boys made poor decisions, I felt sorrow, but I didn't love them less. In fact, in those times I became even more aware of my intense love for them.

Our motivation for not grieving the Holy Spirit should not be born out of religious legalism or fear, but rather out of a heart to honor the One who has given us the great privilege of

---

47   1 John 1:9

hosting His Presence.

God's House Rule #2: Do not quench the Holy Spirit.[48]

The word *quench* means to stifle, but it also means to extinguish a flame. Think back to what you read at the beginning of this chapter about the tongues of fire that settled on each of the believers when they were filled with the Holy Spirit. In the Bible, fire is often a symbol of God the Holy Spirit. That flame of God that burns inside of you is meant to give you guidance and show you which path to walk. When you quench the Holy Spirit, you're making a decision to go on your own and to not follow the leading of the Holy Spirit. That decision almost never turns out well.

I think it's interesting to note the connection between House Rule #2 and House Rule #1. House Rule #1 says to not grieve the Holy Spirit. And if you remember, we grieve the Holy Spirit when we continue in our sin. In Galatians 5:16, Paul shows us the connection between House Rule #1 and House Rule #2:

So I say, let the Holy Spirit guide your lives.
Then you won't be doing what your sinful nature craves.[49]

If you follow House Rule #2, you'll automatically follow House Rule #1. If you yield to the leading of the Holy Spirit, you will not grieve the Holy Spirit.

House Rule #2 is easy to understand, but maybe not quite as easy to follow. It's not easy to give over the leadership of

---

48   1 Thessalonians 5:19
49   New Living Translation

your life after years and years of calling your own shots. You have to humble yourself before God and trust Him for not only your eternal life, but with your life when you wake up tomorrow morning. And the next day. And the next. It might not be easy, but it's totally worth it.

Before you move on to the next chapter, just take a few moments and reflect on the fact that, as a follower of Jesus, you are the dwelling place of God. You are His holy temple. Honor Him with thanks for giving you the privilege of hosting His presence.

TORN

CHAPTER 6

A New Kingdom

From that time Jesus began to preach and say, "Repent, for the kingdom of heaven is at hand."
Matthew 4:17 NASB

When Jesus began His earthly ministry, He immediately began speaking of a new kingdom that would soon arise.[50] He referred to it interchangeably as the kingdom of heaven and the kingdom of God. Jesus made it clear that this new kingdom was not a part of the Old Covenant, but rather an expression of the New Covenant.

The law and the prophets were until John. Since that time the kingdom of God
has been preached, and everyone is pressing into it.
Luke 16:16 NKJV

After decades of oppressive Roman rule, great numbers of people in Israel became very excited at the prospect of a Jewish king re-establishing a Jewish kingdom. If baseball caps had been invented then, they would have all been wearing red ones

---

50   Matthew 4:17

that said "Make Israel Great Again"! The problem is that Jesus wasn't talking about a physical kingdom, and He hadn't come to overthrow any earthly kingdom—at least, not this time around.

But this was no imaginary kingdom. It was real, even though it wasn't readily seen with the naked eye. Jesus said at that time, "The kingdom of God does not come with observation; nor will they say, 'See here!' or 'See there!' For indeed, the kingdom of God is within you."[51]

What Jesus told them then, and is telling us today, is that the kingdom of God is the rule and reign of Jesus in our hearts and minds. This is a real kingdom, with a real flesh-and-blood King and a real citizenship made up of all true believers in Jesus. But unlike earthly kingdoms, this kingdom has no geographical boundaries, and the reign of its King is eternal. Oh, and one more thing—the King of this kingdom is perfect in every way.

Seeing the Unseen

In what seems to be a paradox, Jesus tells us on one hand that the kingdom of God is not observable.[52] But in John 3:3, Jesus told Nicodemus that it *is* possible to see the kingdom of God. So, which is it? Can we see the kingdom, or not?

In His usual form, Jesus is correct in both of His seemingly contradictory statements. It all depends on what you're looking for. If you're looking for a political answer to a spiritual problem, you're not going to see the kingdom of heaven. If you're focusing on building your own kingdom, you won't see the kingdom of God. And most importantly, if you're not born again, you won't see the kingdom of God.

---

51   Luke 17:20-21 NKJV
52   Luke 17:20-21

In my younger years, as I read John 3:3 and Jesus' words about not being able to see the kingdom of God unless we are born again, I interpreted it to mean that if we don't accept Jesus as Savior we won't go to heaven. While that is certainly a biblical truth, it's not entirely what Jesus meant here. Jesus definitely taught us that we need to trust in Him (be born again) in order to live with Him in eternity. He's also saying that if we're born again (saved), we can "see" spiritual realities that are not seen with the physical eye.

The kingdom of heaven is present and active on the earth today. That's also something I didn't understand as a young believer. For some reason, I thought that whenever the Bible talked about the kingdom of heaven, it meant the future time when we're with Jesus in eternity. So, when I prayed the Lord's Prayer,[53] I just assumed that "Your kingdom come" meant that we are praying for the soon return of Jesus to earth. But that's not what that passage of Scripture means. It means that we should be praying for the advancement of His kingdom in the hearts and minds of people all over the earth. It also teaches us how to pray the will of the Father. We know that the Father's will is accomplished in heaven; and in the Lord's Prayer, Jesus teaches us to pray for that same will to be done here on earth.[54] Whenever we see something here on earth that doesn't look like heaven, we are to pray for that situation to come into alignment with God's will. And we know God's will, because we have the Holy Spirit and we know what the will of heaven is.

The Unseen Becoming Visible

There's a big difference between unseen and invisible. If something is invisible, you wouldn't be able to see it even if

---

53   Matthew 6:9-13
54   Matthew 6:10

you tried. But if something's unseen, it just means that you haven't seen it yet. The Bible never says the kingdom of heaven is invisible, but it does say that for many people it remains unseen. However, if we're advancing the kingdom in the way Jesus asked us to, the unseen kingdom of God should begin to be visible even in the realm of the unsaved. Here's what Jesus said in Matthew 10:7-8:

And as you go, preach, saying, "The kingdom of heaven is at hand." Heal the sick, cleanse the lepers, raise the dead, cast out demons.

Matthew 10:7-8a NKJV

The unseen kingdom of heaven becomes visible when we see people being miraculously healed by the power of God. Although I don't keep count, I have personally witnessed probably close to a hundred miraculous healings during my time as a pastor. Two times I prayed for people with visibly broken bones and saw them instantly healed! I prayed for a thirty-two-year-old woman with two herniated discs in her lower back who was so debilitated that she could barely walk, even while using a walker. When I prayed for her, she was instantly healed and remains healed and pain-free to this day. A sixteen-year-old girl in my congregation was blacking out, and a scan showed a black spot on her brain. After I prayed for her, the blackout episodes stopped, and a follow-up scan showed no spots on the brain. I personally know a man and wife from Hawaii whose eight-year-old son drowned while playing in the ocean. After forty-five minutes of unsuccessful revival efforts, the paramedics on the scene pronounced him dead. His lifeless body had already begun to stiffen. His parents, who described themselves as nominal Christians, cried out to Jesus in desperation and pleaded with Him to bring life back into their little boy. Almost immediately, the little boy coughed and sputtered and came back to life!

The point is, many people who witnessed these supernatural miracles had never "seen" the kingdom of heaven. But now here it was, right before their very eyes. The kingdom of God was at hand, and its reality was undeniable. The unseen kingdom became visible.

The Apostle Paul made it very clear in his teachings that God's kingdom is demonstrated through powerful signs and wonders.

> **They were convinced by the power of miraculous signs and wonders and by the power of God's Spirit. In this way, I have fully presented the Good News of Christ from Jerusalem all the way to Illyricum.**
> **Romans 15:19 NLT**

In essence, Paul is saying that if God's power through signs and wonders was not present in his preaching, he would not be presenting the complete gospel. Jesus Himself says that signs and wonders should be a part of the life of all those who believe in Him. In Paul's letter to the Corinthians, he says that the kingdom is not a matter of talk but of power.[55]

Unfortunately, many Christians—and even entire denominations—have discounted the biblical truth that God's supernatural power through signs and wonders should be at work in our lives today. It's important, because that's how people can see the unseen kingdom. If we as Christians don't demonstrate the power of God, many people will never see the kingdom of God. Likewise, if we don't look for the kingdom of God, we'll miss the power of God.

---

55   1 Corinthians 4:20

First Things First

As you read the gospel accounts, it seems as though Jesus was always having to help people get their priorities straight. The same goes for us today. We're quick to say that Jesus is number one in our lives, but oftentimes our actions speak otherwise. So, it should come as no surprise that Jesus has to continually remind us through His Word that we are to first and foremost seek the kingdom of God.[56] What does that even mean?

The word *seek* in the original Greek language of the New Testament means to "try to find" or to "try to obtain." So what Jesus is saying is that the first thing we should be doing as His followers is to operate as citizens of the kingdom of heaven. Sadly, many Christians are so focused on building their own kingdom that they spend very little time advancing the kingdom of God. And because they're not paying attention to the kingdom of God, they're missing out on much of God's supernatural power that could be flowing in and through them.

Politics is an area that can easily divert our attention away from God's kingdom and toward man-made government. I consider myself to be patriotic, and I feel blessed to live in one of the greatest countries to ever exist. But in my observation, I've seen well-meaning Christians devote huge amounts of time and energy in the political arena trying to change laws, but little or no time trying to change hearts. Jesus didn't come to change laws; He came to change hearts. Only when the hearts of our nation are changed will the laws of our nation reflect the character and nature of God. As believers, we need to demonstrate the kingdom of God to our governmental leaders and social influencers.

In a twist of irony, one of the biggest barriers to seeking the kingdom of God is religion. More specifically, I'm talking

---

56   Matthew 6:33

about long-held traditions and rituals that are devoid of any real power from God. There are certain traditions and practices that can draw us closer to God and release His supernatural power in our lives. However, many churches and denominations over the centuries have increasingly turned to man-made traditions and empty rituals that might make people *feel* more religious, but that in reality are doing nothing to advance the kingdom of God in this world. The Bible warns us to avoid religious groups who have a form of godliness but no demonstration of God's supernatural power.[57] You'd like to think that the church would not be a hinderance to people seeking the kingdom of God. And yet week after week, there are churches where those in attendance are largely unaware that the kingdom of heaven is here and is currently in operation. Interestingly, churches and denominations who incorporate some of the Old Covenant into their observances seem to be the ones most apt to miss the current reality of the kingdom of God.

Never Stop Looking

In what appears to be a great paradox, the Bible tells us to be looking for something that is unseen.

So we fix our eyes not on what is seen, but on what is unseen, since what is seen is temporary, but what is unseen is eternal.
2 Corinthians 4:18 NIV

Remember—just because something is unseen doesn't mean it's invisible. It just means you haven't seen it yet. Just like the Jews in the time of Jesus, we may be missing the kingdom because we're looking for the wrong kind of kingdom. You

---

57   2 Timothy 3:5

need to stop looking with your physical eyes and start looking with your spiritual eyes. Yield to the Holy Spirit, and let Him show you what's really going on in the spiritual realm. It's time to step up and take responsibility as a citizen of the kingdom of God.

As this chapter comes to a close, I want you to stop for a minute and assess what you've been focusing on. Where are your eyes fixed? We're all pulled in many different directions in our busy lives. We all have numerous responsibilities that require our attention and concern. But we must not let these things, as important as they are, steal our focus from God's kingdom. Keep on looking for the unseen.

TORN

CHAPTER 7

A New Scapegoat

Scapegoat: [**skeyp**-goht] *a person or group made to bear the blame for others or to suffer in their place*[58]

Even though we're no longer under the Old Covenant, there's great value in studying and understanding it, because it all points to Jesus. There is so much rich symbolism in all the feasts, the priestly duties, and even the physical layout of the tabernacle. One very interesting Old Covenant ordinance actually involved a goat.

Each year on the Day of Atonement (Yom Kippur), the high priest would lay his hands on the head of the goat and confess the sins of the people. This action symbolized the transferring of the sins of the people to the goat. The goat would then be herded out into the wilderness to be seen no more. It was to demonstrate that their sins would be taken away.[59]

The first known use of the word *scapegoat* comes from the Bible.[60] The two Hebrew root words that make up the word *scapegoat* are *goat* and *disappear*. The word *scapegoat* is still commonly used in our language today, and it means "a person or group made to bear the blame for others or to suffer in their place."

---

58   www.dictionary.com
59   Leviticus 16:21-22
60   Leviticus 16:8

Have you ever been a scapegoat? The odds are pretty good that you have, in one way or another. It seems as though our society is increasingly looking for someone to blame. The level of finger-pointing and blame-shifting seems like it's at an all-time high. Everyone makes mistakes, but no one is willing to take the blame.

Well, almost no one.

A Scapegoat in Prophecy

About 700 years before Christ, the prophet Isaiah penned one of the most well-known prophecies concerning Jesus.

> **Yet it was our weaknesses he carried;**
> **it was our sorrows that weighed him down.**
> **And we thought his troubles were a punishment from God,**
> **a punishment for his own sins!**
> **But he was pierced for our rebellion,**
> **crushed for our sins.**
> **He was beaten so we could be whole.**
> **He was whipped so we could be healed.**
> **All of us, like sheep, have strayed away.**
> **We have left God's paths to follow our own.**
> **Yet the Lord laid on him**
> **the sins of us all.**
> **Isaiah 53:4-6 NLT**

Jesus is the New Covenant scapegoat. But this new scapegoat can do something that the old scapegoat could not. He can actually remove our sin. Under the Old Covenant, sins weren't really taken away; they were merely covered until a time when the Messiah would come and take them away. One of the Hebrew root words of *atonement* literally means to *cover*. Jesus doesn't cover our sin; He deletes it. Psalm 103 says that Jesus removed our sin as far as the east is from the west. If you're doing the math, that's infinitely far apart. After 1,500 years of sins being covered but not taken away, you can see why John the Baptist was so excited to see Jesus come on the scene as the One who would take away our sin.[61] A big part of the New Covenant is when God declared that He would no longer remember our sin.[62]

Blameless

Since Jesus is our scapegoat, it means He took the blame for our misdeeds. That being so, where does that leave us? As shocking as this may sound, it leaves you blameless.

> **Yet now he has reconciled you to himself through the death of Christ in his physical body. As a result, he has brought you into his own presence, and you are holy and blameless as you stand before him without a single fault.**
> **Colossians 1:22 NLT**

As believers, we struggle to see ourselves as God sees us. So, for most Christians it might be a stretch to see themselves as holy and blameless. God's Word even goes on to say that we stand before Him without a single fault! Even though this is totally true, it can be hard to wrap our brains around it because we, of all people, know that we have faults. So, how is it that we as faulty people can stand before God as faultless? It's as

61   John 1:29
62   Jeremiah 31:34

simple as this—either Jesus took our sins away, or He didn't.

The hallmark of Christian belief is that Jesus came to take our sins away, and yet many believers still walk around hanging their heads in shame and guilt over their wrongdoing. If Jesus took it away, why is it still there? Could it possibly be that we really don't believe He took it away? Either you believe it, or you don't. If you call yourself a believer, what exactly are you believing in?

Let's try this one more time: Jesus takes your sin away so that you can stand before the Father as holy and blameless. Do you believe it?

It's hard to believe because it sounds too good to be true. That's why it's called the gospel. *Gospel* literally means "good news." It's not good news if you have to try really hard to live righteously, and if you try hard enough, maybe you'll make it to heaven. That's the message of man-made religion, but it's not the message of Jesus Christ. The message of Jesus—the gospel message—is that He takes your sin away so that you can stand before God without a single fault. That's good news! What an amazing Scapegoat we have!

Living Your New Life

A few years ago, I had the opportunity to hear Graham Cooke speak at a local church in my area. I didn't really know much about him, but his English accent and gentle personality kept me comfortably engaged. And then he made a statement that almost made me jump out of my skin and shout, "Heresy!"

This is what he said: "Jesus isn't interested in working on your sin."

That single statement had me looking for my car keys and the exit. But before I gathered up the courage to get up and walk out, he began to explain what he meant. Because I don't have access to his exact words, I will share with you my understanding of his explanation. In the following paragraph I have used an abundance of footnotes in order to remain firmly biblical.

The Bible tells us that when we are saved, our old life is gone and we have begun a new life.[63] In fact, that's exactly what Jesus meant when He said that we must be born again.[64] Paul tells us that we are to consider ourselves dead to sin and alive to Christ.[65] Paul also says that our old life has been crucified with Christ.[66]

So, here's the bottom line: Jesus killed your old life, and He has no interest in digging it back up and trying to fix it. What He *is* interested in is helping you to live your new life. So many well-meaning Christians are spending time and energy trying to fix their old life rather than focusing on living their new life. God's Word clearly tells us that if we live our new life through the power of the Holy Spirit, we won't be walking in our old ways.[67]

A Clear Conscience

It's amazing what a clear conscience will do for a person. Sadly, though, many Christians live every day with a guilty conscience. Mostly it's because they don't totally understand what Jesus did for them on the cross, which, as we discussed earlier, was to make them holy and blameless before God. To make matters even worse, many pastors, and even entire denominations, have used guilt and shame to "keep their flock under control." These so-called leaders would shudder to think that we actually believe that, as believers, we stand holy and

63   2 Corinthians 5:17
64   John 3:3
65   Romans 6:11
66   Romans 6:6, Galatians 2:20
67   Galatians 5:16

blameless before God.

It might be somewhat of a surprise to you that God actually wants you to have a clear conscience. He wants you to have a clear conscience because He wants you in His presence. It's true that God is present everywhere. It's called omnipresence. But we're not talking about God's omnipresence—rather, His *manifest presence*. *Manifest* means "readily perceived by the eye or by understanding, evident, obvious, apparent, plain."[68] So, even though God is everywhere present (omnipresent), His manifest presence is what changes lives. That's why He wants us to enter into that presence. But God knows that if we have a guilty conscience, one of the last things we want to do is to enter into His manifest presence. It's important to God that you understand how He sees you (holy and blameless), so that you can come into His presence with a clear conscience.[69] The writer of Hebrews tells us that the Old Covenant was not sufficient to clear our conscience,[70] and it's only through the perfect sacrifice of Jesus that we can have a clear conscience.[71]

May I suggest that you ask the Holy Spirit to show you how God the Father sees you? Because when you begin to see yourself in the same way that God sees you, you'll be able to get past your past and live your new life with a clear conscience.

---

68   www.dictionary.com
69   Hebrews 10:22
70   Hebrews 9:9
71   Hebrews 9:14

TORN

CHAPTER 8

A New Access

Inside every one of us is an innate sense that there's more to our existence than what we experience in the physical realm. Because of that, we have an inborn desire to transcend our natural surroundings and connect to a higher power. To many people the higher power is still unknown, but as Christians we know who and what the higher power is. We most often refer to Him as God, but because He's a personal God, He gave us His personal name: Yahweh.[72]

Most Bible translations insert the word *Lord* for *Yahweh*, because the ancient Jews felt like the name *Yahweh* was too holy for them to even speak. So when you're reading the Old Testament section of the Bible, whenever you see *Lord* as it refers to God, it's actually the personal pronoun *Yahweh*, which basically means *self-existent*.[73] Some Bible translations use the name Jehovah for Yahweh, which is basically a hybrid word made from the Hebrew words for Yahweh and Lord.[74]

It's important to God to give us His personal name, because He's a personal God. Yahweh is not some far-away God who makes us part of His cosmic ant farm. He's a God who created us to be with Him in a personal way. This idea of a personal God is clearly shown in the Garden of Eden, where Yahweh walked and talked with Adam and Eve on a daily basis.

---

72   Exodus 6:3
73   Strong's Hebrew #3068
74   Harper's Bible Dictionary

But sin interrupted that personal intimacy with God, and from that time until the death of Jesus, personal access to God became very limited.

The Curtain Between God and Mankind

During the Old Covenant, the temple served as a meeting place for God's people, the place where priests made sacrifices on behalf of the people, and the dwelling place of God Himself. The temple was divided into three sections. The first section was the public meeting place and was open to all of God's people. The second section, called the Holy Place, was only open to the priests, and it's where they carried out the sacrifices and other priestly duties. The third section, called the Most Holy Place, was partitioned off by a thick curtain (three to four inches thick) and was where the manifest presence of God was. The high priest was the only person allowed in that room, once per year, on the Day of Atonement.

During the Old Covenant, coming into the presence of God in the Most Holy Place was a very serious matter. If the high priest had not properly cleansed himself (spiritually), he would fall dead in the presence of God. In the case that this would happen, a long rope was tied around the ankle of the high priest and bells were attached to his garment. If the bells quit dinging, that meant the high priest had quit moving, which meant that he had probably died. Since no one else was allowed in the Most Holy Place, the rope around the high priest's ankle was a means of body retrieval. So, as you can see, entering into the presence of God during the Old Covenant was very limited and very serious.

But after 1,500 years of a curtain between God and man, an amazing thing happened on the day Jesus died on the cross. At the moment of His death, the curtain in the temple was torn from top to bottom.[75] This action in the physical realm was a picture of what was happening in the spiritual realm. The death of Christ had opened up access to the presence of God. So, with this new access, who may enter in?

A New Curtain

To be honest, under the New Covenant, there's still a curtain between us and God. That curtain is Jesus.

Therefore, brothers and sisters, since we have confidence to enter the Most Holy Place by the blood of Jesus, by a new and living way opened for us through the curtain, that is, his body.
Hebrews 10:19-20 NIV

Every person on the face of the earth now has access to the Most Holy Place, which is the manifest presence of God. However, there's still a curtain to go through.

Jesus clearly tells us that no one can have access to the Father unless they go through Him.[76] In order to go through Jesus, we must first believe what He says. Believing what Jesus says is not the same as believing that Jesus exists. You can believe that someone exists but not believe what they tell you. Jesus tells you that He's the way, the truth, and the life.[77] Do you believe Him? Jesus tells you that you must be born again. Do you believe Him? Jesus says that He takes your sin away. Do you believe Him? Jesus says that He's the *only* way to the Father. Do you believe Him? There's a word for believing what

---

75   Matthew 27:50-51
76   John 14:6
77   John 14:6

Jesus says. It's called *faith*. Faith in Jesus is your key that gives you access to the Most Holy Place and the manifest presence of God. That key is now available to every person on the face of this planet.

Your Father Is Smiling

Years ago, when our kids were young, my wife Donna and I were snuggled on the living room couch trying to have an adult conversation while our four-year-old son Jayden was bouncing all over us. After several minutes of this, and with Jayden right on top of us, Donna said, "Jayden, what makes you think we want you here?"

Without missing a beat, Jayden smiled and said, "Well... you're smiling!"

It was true. Even though our young son was being somewhat annoying, he had us smiling. And to him, our smile was an invitation for him to come join us.

Did you know that God smiles at you? In several Bible passages it says that God's face shines on us.[78] This can accurately be translated as God smiling at us. There may be many of you thinking that God is definitely not smiling at you right now, because of all the things you've done. If that's you, then you're not remembering how God the Father sees you. He sees you through the lens of what Jesus has done in your life, which is removing your sin. The Father isn't looking at your personal attempt at righteousness; He's looking at the righteousness of Christ in which you are now clothed.[79] That makes Him smile.

God's smile is your invitation to come into His presence. You've been washed clean by the blood of Jesus and stand be-

---

78   Numbers 6:25, Psalm 67:1
79   2 Corinthians 5:21, Galatians 3:27

fore your Father as holy and blameless.[80] Therefore, with a clear conscience, you can now confidently come into the Most Holy Place and the presence of God the Father.

> **Therefore, brothers and sisters, since we have confidence to enter the Most Holy Place by the blood of Jesus, by a new and living way opened for us through the curtain, that is, his body, and since we have a great priest over the house of God, let us draw near to God with a sincere heart and with the full assurance that faith brings, having our hearts sprinkled to cleanse us from a guilty conscience and having our bodies washed with pure water.**
>
> **Hebrews 10:19-22 NIV**

In my younger years, I, like many kids, found ways to provoke my parents to anger. I grew up in a stable home and was never abused, but when I angered my parents—especially my dad—I knew to steer clear of him for a while. If my dad was smiling, I knew it was okay to resume normal relations. If he wasn't smiling, well... maybe I'd just keep my distance from him for a while longer.

Here's a newsflash for some of you: Your Father, God, is not angry with you. His anger against your sin was extinguished on the cross.[81] Your Heavenly Father has not been angry with you in the past, He's not angry with you now, and He won't be angry with you in the future. His wrath toward your sin has been satisfied by the blood of Jesus. He's not frowning at you; He's smiling at you. It's his invitation for you to come into His presence.

---

80   Colossians 1:22
81   Romans 5:9, 1 Thessalonians 5:9

His Life-Changing Presence

God is omnipresent, which means He is present everywhere. But His manifest presence is different than His omnipresence. You may remember from the previous chapter that *manifest* means "readily perceived by the eye or the understanding; evident; obvious; apparent; plain."[82] So, while it's true that God is present everywhere all the time, not everyone is experiencing His presence in a real and tangible way. When you are in the manifest presence of God, you will definitely know it!

I've had years of Bible training, both formal and informal, but nothing has changed my life more than being in the manifest presence of God. I'm not saying that my salvation experience and Bible knowledge have not impacted my life—they have. I guess what I'm trying to say is that being in the manifest presence of God helped the knowledge in my brain go to my heart. It's one thing to *know* something, and quite another to actually *do* something. Spending time in the presence of God has inspired me to do more, because it has deepened my relationship with Him. In the past, my service to God has been motivated more by a sense of duty to Him rather than out of relationship with Him.

Spending time in the presence of God has also changed my appetites. I'm not saying that I no longer do anything wrong; I'm just saying that my desire to do wrong things changed dramatically when I purposefully started spending time in the presence of God. It wasn't even something I was thinking about. In other words, I didn't start out spending time with God as a way to help me curb my sinful habits. But as time went on, I noticed that my appetite for sin had decreased noticeably, and I knew that it came from my time in God's manifest presence.

---

82   www.dictionary.com

I also began to notice that worry and fear had a hard time surviving in the rarefied air of God's personal presence. Like they do for many of you, worry and fear have a way of sneaking into my life and stealing my peace. I've found that the best cure is—you guessed it—the presence of God. I don't want to sound like a broken record, but spending time in the manifest presence of God will change your life in countless ways. Nobody knows this better than the Father Himself, and that's why He invites you into His presence.

Entering In

So, how do you step from the omnipresence of God into the manifest presence of God? I can think of no clearer instruction than Psalm 100.

> **Enter his gates with thanksgiving and his courts with praise.**
> **Psalm 100:4 NIV**

I suppose there are other ways to enter into the manifest presence of God, but praise and worship is certainly the big front door. I've heard it argued both ways on whether it's God coming into our realm, or us coming into His realm. I think it's both.

People through the ages have wondered if the morning dew that appears on the grass fell from the sky or came up from the ground. The answer, at least according to my fifth-grade science teacher, is that dew simply appears when the conditions of temperature and humidity are just right. So, dew doesn't rise, nor does it fall. It appears.

At the risk of pressing this illustration too far, the manifest presence of God is much like the morning dew. It doesn't really rise, and it doesn't really fall; it appears when the conditions are right. So, what are those conditions? I want to be careful not to make this into a "recipe" for experiencing God's presence. However, there are a few things that God's Word says about coming into His presence in the Most Holy Place that have already been mentioned in this chapter.

Here's a quick summary.

First of all, we have to remember that there's still a curtain between us and God. Fortunately, that curtain is Jesus Himself, and He has opened the curtain for you to enter in. Faith in Jesus gives you access to the manifest presence of God.

Secondly, you must see yourself in the same way that God sees you. Because you have been washed by the blood of Jesus, you stand before the Father as holy and blameless. This is an important concept, because if you are filled with guilt and shame, the last place you'll want to be is in the presence of a holy God.

And finally, you enter in through thanksgiving, praise, and worship. Jack Hayford once said that worship liberates us from self. In order for us to come into the presence of God, we must be freed from our self-centeredness so that we can focus on God and His amazing attributes.

There are two important things I've learned regarding coming into God's presence through praise and worship. First of all, you have to be intentional. This stuff doesn't just happen. You have to make a decision to enter into His presence, and then position your heart to offer praise and thanksgiving without reservation or distraction.

The second thing I've learned is that all of this takes time. I'm talking about taking time out of your busy day. I know—you're busy. Everyone's busy. Even people who aren't busy are busy. Just ask them. I get it. But there's no substitution for time.

If you don't purposefully take time to get alone with God, then you can't expect to fully experience His life-changing presence. In my own life, the biggest barrier to experiencing God's manifest presence is time. And when I don't take the time to get alone with God, my life shows it.

I encourage you to make some hard calls in your life and commit to carving out some time to enter into the Most Holy Place, where you can experience the manifest presence of God. These moments of intentional, personal worship have changed my life more than anything else, and I know that they will change your life, too.

TORN

CHAPTER 9

A New Nature

I recently conducted a poll on social media where I asked people who identified themselves as Christian to answer this question: Do followers of Jesus have a sinful nature? Of the respondents, 61 percent answered yes, while 39 percent said no. While this poll is not scientific, it's been my experience that a majority of Christians would agree that followers of Jesus have a sinful nature. What would your answer be? Yes, or no?

Fortunately, the Bible clearly gives us an answer to this important question. But for some reason, many of us have received inaccurate teaching and have drawn unbiblical conclusions regarding our sin nature. Not only did I receive wrong teaching, but for many years as a pastor I taught this wrong teaching! So, what did I teach that was not correct? I taught that everyone has a sinful nature, whether they're believers or not. Everyone. The problem is, that's not true.

What *is* true is the fact that we're all born with a sinful nature. The apostle Paul writes at length about his sinful nature, especially in Romans chapter 7.

> **So then, I myself in my mind am a slave to God's law,
> but in my sinful nature a slave to the law of sin.**
> **Romans 7:25b NIV**

There's no mistaking here that Paul is referring to his sinful nature. For many years I've heard several pastors, teachers, and mature Christians speak about our sinful nature as Christians, and they point to verses like this to prove their point. In fact, almost all of Romans 7 is about Paul's struggle with his sin nature. But—and this is a big but—if you keep reading the last few words of chapter 7, and then continue onto chapter 8, you'll see that Paul is talking about his sinful nature in the past tense.

Paul says in the last few words of Romans 7 that in his sinful nature, he is a slave to the law of sin.[83] As followers of Jesus Christ under the New Covenant, are we still slaves to the law of sin? The answer is a resounding "No!" As you continue reading in Romans 8, Paul says, "Because through Christ Jesus the law of the Spirit who gives life has set you free from the law of sin and death."[84]

Once again, just to be clear, Paul is basically saying that if you have a sinful nature, you're a slave to sin. And then he goes on to point out that through Jesus, we are set free from the law of sin. So, let's connect the dots. Without Jesus, you have a sinful nature and are subject to the law of sin. But if you are a follower of Jesus, you have been set free from the law of sin and your sinful nature.

I'm just going to come right out and say it. Followers of Jesus no longer have a sinful nature. That doesn't mean that Christians can't sin; it just means that it's not our nature. Still need more convincing?

Throw off your old sinful nature and your former way of life, which is corrupted by lust and deception. Instead, let the Spirit renew your thoughts and attitudes. Put on your new nature, created to be like God—truly righteous and holy.
Ephesians 4:22-24 NLT

---

83   Romans 7:25
84   Romans 8:2 NIV

True followers of Jesus have a new nature—not a sin nature.

When I was a young adult and working at my first full-time job, I was driving through city traffic with a co-worker when suddenly, a driver darted out in front of me and cut me off. I shouted angrily and shook my fist as the car sped away in front of me. My co-worker turned to me and said, "Mike, that's not your nature!"

She was right. That wasn't my nature. I'm not normally one who lashes out at other people—but I did. I wish I could say that was the only time I reacted in anger, but it's not. There have been a few times since then that I have acted out of character and lashed out in anger. However, those actions aren't part of my nature. I guess what I'm trying to say is that it's possible to sin and not have a sinful nature. Jesus has set me free from my old sin nature, *and* He forgives me of the sins I commit that go against my new nature.

Where the Old Covenant Fell Short

The Old Covenant (the Law) was given for several important reasons, one of which was to make us aware of our own sin.[85] Most of what Paul was writing about in Romans 7 talks about his struggle with sin under the Law. In essence, Paul says that while the Law was effective at making us aware of our sin, it had no power to free us from our nature to sin. That's why it's so important to keep reading at the end of Romans 7 and go into Romans 8.

> **For what the law was powerless to do because it was weakened by the flesh, God did by sending his own Son in the likeness of sinful flesh to be a sin offering. And so he condemned sin in the flesh, in order that the righteous requirement of the law might be fully met in us, who do not live according to the flesh but according to the Spirit.**
>
> **Romans 8:3-4 NIV**

---

85   Romans 7:7

Before the New Covenant, only certain people were empowered by the Holy Spirit, and even then it was only for a limited time. As beneficiaries of the New Covenant, we now have 24/7 access to the Holy Spirit. The Bible makes it abundantly clear that our new nature is lived out as we follow the leading of the Holy Spirit.

But now, by dying to what once bound us, we have been released from the law so that we serve in the new way of the Spirit, and not in the old way of the written code.
Romans 7:6 NIV

I personally know far too many Christians who struggle with trying to follow the written code (the Law) and then blame their sin nature when they fall short. And that's the problem when we mix the obsolete Old Covenant with the New Covenant. First of all, we're supposed to be following the Holy Spirit, and not the Law. Secondly, as New Covenant believers, we're not supposed to have a sin nature. But week after week, month after month, year after year, many preachers and teachers exhort us to follow the Law and continually remind us of our sinful nature. It's no wonder so many Christians are confused. Instead, the Bible exhorts us to follow the leading of the Holy Spirit and embrace our new nature.

Your New Nature

This means that anyone who belongs to Christ has become a new person. The old life is gone; a new life has begun!
2 Corinthians 5:17 NLT

The term "born again" has almost become a cliché. That's unfortunate, because our life as a Christian should be about living our new life in Christ, and it's impossible to live that new life without being born again. By the way, Jesus is the one who coined the phrase "born again."[86] If that phrase is important to Jesus, then it should be important to us. It's important to Jesus because it clearly illustrates that our old life has gone, and a new life has come. With that new life comes a new nature that has been given to us by God Himself. And because God gives this new nature to us through the Holy Spirit, it's a *divine* nature.

> **His divine power has given us everything we need for a godly life through our knowledge of him who called us by his own glory and goodness. Through these he has given us his very great and precious promises, so that through them you may participate in the divine nature, having escaped the corruption in the world caused by evil desires.**
>
> **2 Peter 1:3-4 NIV**

You can either have a sinful nature or a divine nature, but you can't have both. God has given you everything you need to have a divine nature—a nature of holiness and righteousness. As Christians, we should be focusing on our new divine nature and quit trying to resurrect our old sinful nature.

I have been crucified with Christ,[87] and I am to consider myself dead to sin.[88] As I mentioned earlier, Jesus isn't interested in "fixing" my old sin nature, because He killed it. If I ask Jesus to "fix" my sin, I'm in essence asking Him to dig up what's dead and buried. Jesus didn't die to fix our old life; He died to give us a new life. What Jesus *is* interested in is helping us live our new life. We can't live our new life and our old life at the

---

86   John 3:3, 7
87   Galatians 2:20
88   Romans 6:11

same time. In other words, God is not interested in fixing your junk. He's interested in you living your new life and walking in your divine nature.

A New Label

I don't know how many times I've heard Christians say, "I'm just a sinner saved by grace!" My question to them would be this: Do you mean that you were a sinner before you were saved, or are you saying that you're a sinner now? One of the two possible answers is biblical, and the other is not.

It's biblically correct to say that everyone is a sinner before they accept Jesus as Savior. So, it would be accurate to say that you *were* a sinner, but now you have been saved by grace. However, if you are born again (saved), your label is no longer "sinner." I'm not saying that you won't sin; I'm just saying that "sinner" is no longer your label.

According to the Bible, your label as a born-again believer is "saint." I understand how that label might be challenging to many of you who were brought up being taught that there are only a few saints, who lived long ago and who had to be officially approved as a saint by the "church." I'm sorry to burst your long-held bubble, but every true believer in Jesus is officially a saint. Whenever Paul was addressing Christians, he often referred to them as saints.[89] The word *saint* literally means "holy one." You're not a holy one because of your own good works. You are a holy one because the blood of Christ makes you holy.

---

89   Romans 1:7

> **Or do you not know that wrongdoers will not inherit the kingdom of God? Do not be deceived: Neither the sexually immoral nor idolaters nor adulterers nor men who have sex with men nor thieves nor the greedy nor drunkards nor slanderers nor swindlers will inherit the kingdom of God. And that is what some of you were. But you were washed, you were sanctified, you were justified in the name of the Lord Jesus Christ and by the Spirit of our God.**
> **1 Corinthians 6:9-11 NIV**

I'm not a fan of labels. Occasionally, someone will ask me if I'm a dispensationalist or a non-dispensationalist, a charismatic or an evangelical, a pre-millennialist or a post-millennialist. I usually just say I'm a Christ-follower and leave it at that. But people generally love to label people—except for themselves. Maybe you've had some labels in your lifetime. Maybe you were labeled a tramp, a drunk, a thief, or a liar. But if you have received salvation from Jesus Christ, none of those are your label now. Your only label now comes from God, and He calls you a saint. In 1 Corinthians 6:11, Paul says that you were sanctified. The word *sanctified* means "to be made holy." It's very closely related to the word *saint*. If you're sanctified, you're "saint-i-fied."

So, your label as a believer is no longer a sinner, but rather a saint. It doesn't mean that you don't ever sin, it just means that it's not who you are. It's who you *were*, but not who you *are*, because you now have a new life and a new nature.

A New Way of Thinking

While I greatly appreciate deep theological philosophies, I tend to be more of a how-to guy. At some point, we need to put what we know into action. So, what have you learned from this chapter? It's my hope that you have learned that as followers of Christ, we no longer have a sin nature, but rather a new and divine nature. Additionally, we're now referred to as saints, and not as sinners. So, how do you start living your new life and walking in your new nature?

You were taught, with regard to your former way of life, to put off your old self, which is being corrupted by its deceitful desires; to be made new in the attitude of your minds; and to put on the new self, created to be like God in true righteousness and holiness.
Ephesians 4:22-24 NIV

This section of God's Word tells us that you're made new in the attitude of your mind. In other words, if you want to start living your new life and your new nature, you need to think differently. Instead of thinking of yourself as a dreadful sinner with an inescapable sin nature, you should think of yourself as a saint (holy one) who has a new nature that looks like the nature of God.

For as he thinks within himself, so he is.
Proverbs 23:7 NASB

The first step in changing your life is changing your mind.

Don't copy the behavior and customs of this world, but let God transform you into a new person by changing the way you think.
Romans 12:2a NLT

The word *transform,* in Romans 12:2, is closely related to our English word *metamorphosis,* which means "to undergo a complete change." The example of metamorphosis that we all learned in elementary school is that of a caterpillar transforming into a butterfly. I remember looking into a mason jar at that big, fat caterpillar resting in a nest of leaves and grass and thinking, "There's no way that thing will ever be a butterfly!" But sure enough, several weeks later we came to school and found a beautiful butterfly in that same mason jar that had formerly held the pudgy caterpillar. Amazing!

God wants you to have a major transformation in your life, and it starts by changing the way you think about yourself. You have to understand that through Christ, you now have a new life. You're a new person! You can't keep thinking about the past and dredging up your old life. You also have to understand that you have a new nature, and that your old sin nature is dead and buried.

In the same way, count yourselves dead to sin but alive to God in Christ Jesus.
Romans 6:11 NIV

I think it's also important to note here that your new nature is initiated and lived out by the transforming power of the Holy Spirit, and not by religious rituals and legalism. I've known more than a few Christians who are very dedicated to their religious practices but have not yielded to the Holy Spirit and allowed Him to transform their nature. Paul addressed a similar situation in the Galatian church. Many of the Galatians had confessed Christ as Savior and had started living their new life, but for some reason they began to mix much of the Old Covenant Law into their life as a New Covenant believer. Before long they were nit-picking each other for not adhering to certain Old Testament laws. Near the end of his letter to them, he wrote this brief and poignant statement:

It doesn't matter whether we have been circumcised or not. What counts is whether we have been transformed into a new creation.

Galatians 6:15 NLT

Under the Old Covenant, circumcision was an important sign of religious adherence to the Law. Unfortunately, many early Christians were like the Pharisees in that they were more concerned about outward religious appearances than an inward change of the heart. It's still much the same way today. Don't be fooled into believing that an abundance of religious activity in your life is evidence of your new nature. Far too many Christians fall into that trap. It's nothing new. It's been happening for 2,000 years.

Your new life and your new nature are available now. You don't have to try harder or learn more. After accepting Jesus as Savior, you need to do just two things. First, you must change the way you think. You can no longer think you have a sinful nature. You can no longer call yourself a sinner. The Bible says that you are holy and blameless in the eyes of God[90] and that He has made you a saint. When you begin to think this way, you'll begin to act this way.

Secondly, you must yield to the leading of the Holy Spirit. It's the Holy Spirit that transforms you, not your own efforts. Paul tells us that if we walk in the Holy Spirit, we won't be doing things that go against our new, divine nature.[91] That means you can't call the shots. You now have to allow the Holy Spirit to make the call.

Over time, as you listen to the leading of the Holy Spirit,

90   Colossians 1:22
91   Galatians 5:16

you'll be able to respond almost instinctively to any situation in a godly way, because you will have learned the will and the way of God.

It's time to look forward and not backward. It's time to see yourself the same way God sees you. It's time to throw off your old nature and put on your new nature. It's time to start living your new life.

TORN

CHAPTER 10

A New Position

What's your position? That question could have many different answers, depending the context in which it's asked. I could be asking about your opinion on a certain subject. Maybe I'm asking you where you are physically located. If were talking about the stock market, I might be wanting to know if you're buying or selling. Perhaps we're talking about your employment, and I'm wondering what job you hold in your company. Maybe I'm trying to figure out if you're financially stable or unstable. The word *position* can mean a lot of things, but one thing is for sure: we all want to know what our position is.

But what about your position as a believer in Jesus Christ? Have you ever thought about that? If not, you should, because your position in Christ is multi-faceted and very important.

As the Old Covenant came to a close and the New Covenant was being unveiled, a significant shift happened in the lives of those who followed Jesus. They went from being *around* Jesus to being *in* Jesus.[92] That's a big change in position! And it didn't just happen with the first followers of Jesus; it happened to you, too! The moment that you put your faith in Jesus as your Savior, your position changed. You went from being around Jesus to being *in* Jesus. As Christians, we often talk about Jesus being in us, but we seem to talk less about us being in Jesus. The ramifications of our new position in Jesus are far-reaching and largely untapped by most Christians.

92   John 14:20

Re-Location

Forty days after Jesus' resurrection, He ascended into heaven and is seated with God the Father.[93] But because we are in Jesus, we, too, are seated with God in the heavenly realm. I know; it almost sounds ludicrous that we're seated with Jesus in heaven, especially given that fact that we're still physically here on earth. But God's Word clearly places us in that position.

And God raised us up with Christ and seated us with him in the heavenly realms in Christ Jesus.
Ephesians 2:6 NIV

This scripture isn't talking about a future time after we die; it's talking about the present reality in every believer's life! Obviously, this is not referring to our physical location, but rather to a position of spiritual access.

Perhaps this illustration may help. If you are standing in a store, you're either a customer or an employee. Even though both the customer and the employee are in the same physical position, their position of authority is quite different. The customer has no authority to start rearranging merchandise on the shelves or to run the cash register, but the employee does. We're certainly not an employee of heaven, but we are able to act from a position of authority because of our position in Jesus.

One of the clearest examples of our authority in Christ is found in Luke 10:19, where Jesus tells us that He has given us authority over the devil and every power of the enemy. Jesus also gave us authority over sickness and disease as part of his command to heal the sick and cleanse the lepers.[94]

If we, as believers, are going to advance the kingdom of

---

93   Ephesians 1:20
94   Matthew 10:1, 8

God here on earth, then we must be aware of the authority we have because of our position in Christ. Additionally, we also must be aware of our spiritual location as we walk in our God-given authority. In other words, we need to understand that we're operating from heaven to earth, instead of from earth to heaven. So many Christians view themselves as standing here on earth and crying up to heaven, hoping that God will hear them and maybe shake something loose. The more biblical view is to see ourselves seated in the heavenly realms next to the One who has the power to turn on the pipeline from heaven to earth. In fact, Jesus even taught us to pray that way in the Lord's Prayer, when He said we should pray that God's will in heaven would be done here on earth.[95] The direction of our prayers is to be from heaven to earth, not earth to heaven.

> **I will give you the keys of the kingdom of heaven; and whatever you bind on earth shall have been bound in heaven, and whatever you loose on earth shall have been loosed in heaven.**
> **Matthew 16:19 NASB**

When Jesus told us that He was giving us the keys to the kingdom of heaven, He was letting us know that we should exercise authority in His name here on earth. There are things on this earth that need to be let loose. In the name of Jesus, we should be "loosing" things like love, hope, peace, joy, and good health. But before we loose them on earth, we must first know that they have been loosed in heaven. In other words, it has to be the will of heaven first before it can be a reality on earth.

It's the same idea when it comes to binding. There are things on this earth that need to be bound, like hate, dissension, greed, immorality, sickness, and the work of the devil. We have been given authority by Jesus to bind these kinds of things, but we must first know that they are bound in heaven.

---

95   Matthew 6:10

On earth as it is in heaven.

I'm guessing that for many of you, these last few paragraphs have challenged some long-held ideas and beliefs. These biblical truths challenged me as well. It took a while for me to really grasp what it meant to be seated in the heavenly realms with Jesus, and how that should be carried out in my everyday life. I think as you read the rest of this chapter, some things might start to clear up for you.

A New Citizenship and a New Responsibility

Because you're a part of the kingdom of God, you now have dual citizenship. You're a citizen of this world, but you're also a citizen of heaven,[96] even though you're not physically living there. My friend, Dale, lives and works in the United States, but he's a citizen of Canada. You live and work here in this world, but your real citizenship is in heaven.

There are privileges that come with citizenship, but there are also responsibilities. One of the biggest responsibilities God has given us as citizens in His kingdom is to act as an ambassador.[97] An ambassador is one who is an authorized messenger or representative from one government to another. As a follower of Jesus, you are His ambassador, and you represent His kingdom here on earth. Your residence is here, but your citizenship is in the kingdom of heaven.

It's important to note here that every nation always supplies its ambassadors with what they need to do their job. It's no different in the kingdom of heaven. God promises to provide all that you need in order to carry out all that He's asked of you.[98]

And what has God asked of you as His ambassador? He's asked you to heal the sick, cleanse the lepers, raise the dead,

---

96   Philippians 3:20
97   2 Corinthians 5:20
98   Philippians 4:19

and cast out demons.[99] He's asked you to go make disciples.[100] He's asked you to help reconcile people back to Himself.[101] In essence, He's asked you to do what Jesus did[102]—except for the dying on the cross part.

God will supply everything you need to do what we've just mentioned. It's like a pipeline from heaven to earth, with one very important feature. This pipeline has a valve, and that valve is faith.

Several years ago, I learned that God's power doesn't flow from heaven to earth because of need, but because of faith. That's not to say that God doesn't care about our needs, because He cares deeply. But for whatever reason, in His sovereignty He has chosen to use our faith as the vehicle that moves His power from heaven to earth. Some of you might be wincing a bit from this idea, but let me prove it to you.

What is mankind's greatest need? The answer is salvation. Without salvation, what else matters? How do we receive salvation? The answer is by faith. The answer is *not* need. If God's saving power flowed from heaven because of need, everyone would be saved, because everyone needs salvation. But we all know that not everyone is saved. That's because we're saved by our faith in Jesus. God's power flows because of faith.

Here's another one. How are we healed? The answer is by faith. When you read the gospel accounts of Jesus healing people, He often tells them that their faith has healed them. If God healed people because of need, everyone would be healed. But need is not what causes God's power to flow; it's faith. Get the picture? Our needs are important to God, but it's our faith that He uses as the conduit to fill those needs.

So, back to the point I made earlier. God gives us everything we need to do what He's asked us to do as His ambassadors, but the supply pipeline has a valve, and that valve is your faith. Your faith is what causes God's power to flow from

---

99   Matthew 10:8

100   Matthew 28:19

101   2 Corinthians 5:19

102   John 14:6

heaven to earth. Our job as ambassadors of the kingdom is to spot situations here on earth that don't look like heaven, and then to open a pipeline from heaven to earth for God's power to flow and for the will of heaven to be done here on earth.

A New Focus

It's so easy to be focused on this natural world and all its trappings, but God's Word encourages us to keep things in the right perspective.

Since you have been raised to new life with Christ, set your sights on the realities of heaven, where Christ sits in the place of honor at God's right hand. Think about the things of heaven, not the things of earth.
Colossians 3:1-2 NLT

When you first read this scripture, you might take away the idea that we should be focusing on a future time when we're in eternity in heaven, instead of focusing on the things of this world. While this thought is not necessarily wrong, it's probably not what Paul had in mind when he wrote it. What he probably had in mind was the same encouragement he gave to the Ephesian church when he told them that, as believers, we are seated in the heavenly realms with Jesus. Just as he had encouraged the Ephesians to change their perspective, he now gives that same advice to the Colossians. And because these words are included in God's Word, the same advice extends to you as well.

In another section of scripture, Paul tells us that instead of conforming to this world, we need to be transformed to be more like Jesus. In order for that to happen, we need to change the way we think.[103] We're usually thinking about all the intertwined and sometimes messy situations in our everyday life here on earth, but the Bible says we should spend more time looking at things from the perspective of our position in Christ in the heavenly realm. The first thing we must do in order for that to happen is to change the way we think. The renewed mind is one that thinks more from the supernatural, heavenly perspective than from the natural, worldly perspective.

The world needs Jesus, and since you are His ambassador, the world needs you, too. But for you to be effective as His representative you need to know your position, and your position is a lot more powerful than you probably previously thought.

---

103   Romans 12:2

TORN

CHAPTER 11

A New Generosity

Over the years, many truths in God's Word have been twisted or completely ignored by people who want to accommodate their own agenda and lifestyle. This is especially true in regard to what the Bible has to say about money, and more specifically about the giving of our personal finances to the local church.

You've probably heard many non-churchgoers say "The church only wants my money" as their excuse for not attending church. Unfortunately, a very small but very vocal minority of churches and para-church ministries have given some traction to this attitude. Consequently, many pastors are hesitant to teach about money because they don't want to add fuel to the fire of the "they only want my money" argument. Because of this lack of teaching, most Christians are a little fuzzy about what God has to say regarding our financial responsibilities under the New Covenant.

Since the time of Jesus, many pastors and churches have taught some form of the concept of tithing, in which church members give ten percent of their income to the local church. The word *tithe* literally means "ten percent" and can be found in both the Old and New Testaments. More recently, however, some pastors and many YouTubers are teaching that tithing is limited to the Old Covenant, to which we are no longer bound. Is that true? Are followers of Jesus free from the obligation to tithe? If so, do we have any financial responsibility to the local church?

Before we dive into the controversy of whether or not tithing is for believers today, I want to share with you a clear and concise teaching from the New Testament:

Since you excel in so many ways—in your faith, your gifted speakers, your knowledge, your enthusiasm, and your love from us—I want you to excel also in this gracious act of giving.
2 Corinthians 8:7 NLT

If you study the context in which Paul wrote this verse, you'll see that he was clearly talking about followers of Christ and their responsibility to give financially to the work of the church. And not only to give, but to *excel* in their giving. The word *excel*, as it's used here, means "to go over and above—to give abundantly." Like it or not, God's Word is crystal clear that we, as followers of Christ, under the New Covenant are called to give generously to the work of the local church.

So, what does being a generous New Covenant giver look like?

The History of Tithing

In order for us to have an idea of what financial giving under the New Covenant should look like, we need to have an understanding of what giving, and more specifically tithing, looked like in the Old Testament, including the Law (Old Covenant). The reason we need to understand Old Testament tithing in order to understand New Testament giving will become clear in a moment, so please bear with me.

The concept of tithing was introduced hundreds of years before the Old Covenant Law. In Genesis 14, Abraham voluntarily gave Melchizedek, who was a type and shadow of Jesus, ten percent of what he had just gained in his recent conquest. Decades later, Abraham's grandson, Jacob, is recorded as giving a tithe to God at his place of worship.[104] So, the concept of tithing to God was introduced long before it became a requirement in the Law.[105]

While there are several reasons God instituted tithing in the Old Testament, one important reason was to support the priests in their full-time work of the ministry and to fund the day-to-day operation of the tabernacle, and later on the temple.[106]

Perhaps the most quoted scripture regarding tithing is from the Old Testament prophet, Malachi.

"Will a mere mortal rob God? Yet you rob me. But you ask, 'How are we robbing you?' In tithes and offerings. You are under a curse—your whole nation—because you are robbing me. Bring the whole tithe into the storehouse, that there may be food in my house. Test me in this," says the Lord Almighty, "and see if I will not throw open the flood-gates of heaven and pour out so much blessing that there will not be room enough to store it."
Malachi 3:8-10 NIV

What's interesting about this portion of scripture is that both sides of the tithing argument use it to make their point. Those who say tithing is for today point to this passage as clear biblical proof that all people of God should be tithing; and furthermore, God will bless you if you do and curse you if you don't. Those who say that tithing is not for today point out that this passage of scripture is from the Law, which we are no longer under. They also say that God doesn't curse us under the New Covenant, because Jesus became our curse on the cross.

So, who is correct?

Well, they are both partially correct. That means they're

---

104   Genesis 28:22
105   Leviticus 27:30
106   Numbers 18:21

also partially wrong. Let's see what God's Word has to say about it.

New Covenant Giving

We already read at the beginning of this chapter that under the New Covenant, we're called to be generous givers to the local church. But Paul goes into even more detail:

> **On the first day of every week, each one of you should set aside a sum of money in keeping with your income, saving it up, so that when I come no collections will have to be made.**
> **1 Corinthians 16:2 NIV**

As followers of Jesus under the New Covenant, we should be giving to the church on a regular basis. Furthermore, the Bible says we should give a percentage of our income. But no percentage is listed here. So how much of our income should we be giving?

You may recall that in chapter two of this book, we discovered that the New Covenant actually holds us to a higher standard than the Old Covenant. It's true that we're no longer under the Law, with all of its rules and regulations; but it's also true that under the New Covenant, the Holy Spirit leads us to go above and beyond the requirements of the Law.

So, while it's true that there's no exact percentage given in the New Testament regarding our giving to the local church, based on the context of the New Covenant it would seem reasonable to conclude that ten percent is a minimum baseline to work from.

A Faith-Builder

There are many reasons why God wants you to give the

first portion of your income to the local church. One obvious reason is because it's the main funding source for the day-to-day operation of the church. However, a less obvious but probably more important reason is that giving the first portion of your income to the church builds your faith.

In the last chapter, we stated the important role that your faith plays in the advancement of God's kingdom here on earth. Without God's people stepping out in faith, not much happens. So, how can God train us to have a stronger faith? The answer is through money. Money is something everyone must handle on a consistent basis. So, what better teaching tool is there than money?

Most people can barely live on 100 percent of what they make. So, how in the world are we supposed to survive on 90 percent? The answer is faith. Do you trust God enough to believe that He can enable you to live on what you have left after you give Him 10 percent? Either you do trust Him, or you don't. He wants to show Himself faithful to you when you are faithful to Him. Furthermore, He wants to see if you'll be faithful to Him with your money before He trusts you with more important things of His kingdom.

If you are faithful in little things, you will be faithful in large ones. But if you are dishonest in little things, you won't be honest with greater responsibilities. And if you are untrustworthy about worldly wealth, who will trust you with the true riches of heaven?
Luke 16:10-11 NLT

All of our married life, my wife and I have given at least ten percent of our income to God through the local church. There were times when that was extremely difficult, but we continued to walk in faith through the giving of our finances. I'm not sure how the math worked out, but God *always* took care of us. Sometimes in miraculous ways. When we're faithful to Him with our "little," He's faithful to us with His "much."

The Reason for Financial Blessing

It's unfortunate that a small, but vocal minority of Christian ministries have twisted the biblical truth of sowing and reaping and manipulated good-hearted people into supporting their life-style of greed and excess. God taught me many years ago that abuse of biblical truth does not invalidate biblical truth. And the principle of sowing and reaping is solidly biblical. It's also solidly biblical that God wants to bless you financially. Here's why:

Remember this—a farmer who plants only a few seeds will get a small crop. But the one who plants generously will get a generous crop. You must each decide in your heart how much to give. And don't give reluctantly or in response to pressure. "For God loves a person who gives cheerfully." And God will generously provide all you need. Then you will always have everything you need and plenty left over to share with others. For God is the one who provides seed for the farmer and then bread to eat. In the same way, he will provide and increase your resources and then produce a great harvest of generosity in you. Yes, you will be enriched in every way so that you can always be generous.
2 Corinthians 9:6-8, 10-11a NLT

In case you missed it, God wants to bless your financial giving by giving you more financial resources, so that you can be even more generous! God wants to bless you so that you can be a blessing.

Sadly, many Christians are missing out on the financial blessings that come from sowing and reaping, because they're eating their seed. The scripture above says that God provides financial resources (such as a job) so that you can have money to live on and money to give back to Him through the local church. But when you spend everything you make and don't give any back to Him, you're eating your own seed. And you can't sow if you don't have any seed. You can either eat the seed or sow the seed. But one thing is for sure, you'll reap what you sow.

TORN

CHAPTER 12

A New Sabbath

A few years ago, my wife and I traveled to Israel and spent ten days touring the areas where Jesus walked and taught. It was amazing—and in some ways, life-changing—to see the places where ancient biblical history was played out. One of those life-changing moments in the Holy Land happened in a very unlikely place. It happened in the men's restroom of a modern hotel where we had stopped for lunch. While standing at the urinal, I saw a sign on the wall directly in front of me that read:

> *"Dear Guests, this facility causes a desecration of the Sabbath.*
> *Have a pleasant stay.*
> *The Hotel Management."*

I know that I'm no Hebrew scholar, but I have studied the Bible for many years. For the life of me, I couldn't make any connection between using the restroom and causing a desecration of the Sabbath. Because I'm not one to get caught up in the legalism of the Old Covenant and the laws of the Pharisees, I finished my business in the restroom without a hint of guilt. I was, however, very curious about the sign, so I asked our Jewish tour guide how my use of the men's urinal desecrated the Sabbath.

"Did the urinal have an electric eye for the automatic

flush?" he asked.

"Yes," I answered.

"Well, then, that's why."

What? How in the world does an electric eye that automatically flushes a urinal make me a Sabbath-breaker?

To answer this question, we have to go back to the Old Covenant law that prohibited starting a fire on the Sabbath.[107] You could keep a fire going from the day before, but because actually building a fire was considered work, you couldn't do it and still keep the Sabbath law. Okay, fair enough. No fire-building on the Sabbath.

Then, along came the gasoline-powered automobile, with its internal combustion engine. This presented a problem for modern-day Jews who were not only trying to live up to the Law of Moses, but also to the hundreds of other legalistic demands that had crept into Judaism over the years. So, how did a car cause so much trouble?

An automobile is powered by a series of small explosions, caused when the spark plug emits a spark and ignites a fuel-air mixture inside the cylinders of the engine. So, by Jewish reasoning, if you start an engine, you're starting a fire. During our visit to Israel we noticed that the traffic on Saturday was very light, because only the backslidden Jews would be driving. Sabbath-keeping Jews can walk a mile or two to the synagogue on Saturday, but they can't drive, because they'd be starting a fire.

While in Israel, we also noticed that on the Sabbath, the elevators in buildings would automatically stop on every floor. *Every* floor, no matter how tall the building was. Why? Because when you press the elevator button, you complete an electrical circuit that powers the elevator up and down. Not so much now, but back in the early days of electricity, a spark could

107   Exodus 35:1

be emitted when an electrical connection was made. What's a spark? Well, in a way, it's a form of fire. So, when you press a button that's electrical, according to legalistic Sabbath-keepers, you're starting a fire. That's why the elevators in Israel stop on every floor during the twenty-four hours of the Sabbath. If you get in the elevator and punch a button, you're starting a fire. Most of the newer buildings in Israel have two sets of elevators for use on the Sabbath. One set stops on every floor for the Orthodox Jews and the other set, known as the "Gentile" elevator, operates normally every day of the week. Lucky for us.

So now we can finally get to the desecration of the Sabbath by using a toilet with an electric eye for the flushing mechanism. You're probably already ahead of me. When you approach a toilet with an electric eye an electrical connection is made, so that when you walk away the toilet automatically flushes. Convenient, right? Except that you're starting a fire, and we all know by now that any God-fearing person would never start a fire on the Sabbath. So, if you ever find yourself in Israel on the Sabbath and you have to use the restroom, please look for the old-fashioned toilet with the flush handle because, you know... fire.

You might be wondering by now why I took so long to tell this story. It's because through all of this, I began to see why Jesus had to challenge the Jews of His day regarding their view of the Sabbath. He was saddened and dismayed that their zeal for the Law had perverted their sense of love and justice. In a way, the Pharisees had pushed the line in making the Sabbath an idol. Jesus had to remind them of an important truth regarding the Sabbath.

Then Jesus said to them, "The Sabbath was made to meet the needs of people, and not people to meet the requirements of the Sabbath."
Mark 2:27 NLT

Two thousand years ago, Jesus witnessed a heavy burden of religious legalism that still exists today, particularly in regard to the Sabbath.

The New Covenant Sabbath

A question that many Christians ponder is whether or not we, as New Covenant believers, are bound to the Old Covenant law regarding the Sabbath.[108] If you'll remember back to the beginning of this book, we saw that the Bible clearly states that we are no longer under the Old Covenant Law.[109] Despite what the Bible clearly says, there are many Christians who adamantly believe that we are still required to observe a specific day as the Sabbath, along with many of its rules and regulations.

Therefore do not let anyone judge you by what you eat or drink, or with regard to a religious festival, a New Moon celebration or a Sabbath day. These are a shadow of the things that were to come; the reality, however, is found in Christ.
Colossians 2:16-17 NIV

While we are no longer under the rules and regulations of the Old Covenant Sabbath, there is, however, a New Covenant Sabbath.

There remains, then, a Sabbath-rest for the people of God; for anyone who enters God's rest also rests from their works, just as God did from his.
Hebrews 4:9-10 NIV

---

108   Exodus 20:8-10
109   Hebrews 8:13

The New Covenant Sabbath is not a day; it's a person. Jesus Christ is our Sabbath Rest. Just as Paul wrote in Colossians 2:17, the Old Covenant Sabbath has found its reality in Jesus. That's not to say that we don't need physical rest—we do. Purposefully planning times of physical rest in your week is healthy, wise, and biblical. But Jesus teaches us that our greatest need for rest is for our souls.

Come to me, all you who are weary and burdened, and I will give you rest. Take my yoke upon you and learn from me, for I am gentle and humble in heart, and you will find rest for your souls. For my yoke is easy and my burden is light.
Matthew 11:28-30 NIV

Your soul is that invisible part of you that is your mind, will, intellect, personality, and the seat of your emotions. A soul without rest is known as a *restless* soul. When your soul is restless you may experience anxiety, fear, worry, despair, anger, bitterness, negativity, and a host of other issues. It's safe to say that we all experience some of these things from time to time, but it's not God's intention that this be a way of life for you. Jesus not only came to die for you and give you eternal life in heaven, He also came to give you rest for your soul in this life on earth. He *is* your Sabbath Rest, and you don't have to wait for a particular day to experience the rest He offers.

So how do you enter into that place of rest for your soul that Jesus promised?

Come

The first word that Jesus uses as he invites us into His sabbath rest is *come*.[110] Please notice that His first word is not *do*. So many people are busy *doing* things to try to satisfy their restless soul, rather than just simply *coming* into the presence of Jesus. When Jesus says to come to Him, He's not just referring to a one-time salvation experience, although that's a necessary first step in coming to Him. He's talking about connecting with Him through your spirit on a personal level. It's helpful to remember that Jesus said He actually lives within us,[111] He speaks to us,[112] He shows himself to us,[113] and He longs to visit with us.[114]

Jesus died so that you could be *with* Him, not just in heaven someday in the future, but right here, right now, every day. You can go to church every Sunday and still not be coming to Jesus. You can know the Bible inside and out and still not be coming to Jesus. Coming to Jesus means to purposefully take time to step into His presence and listen to His voice. When Jesus tells you to come to Him, it's an invitation to an ongoing lifestyle and not just an occasional event.

Take

After we come into the presence of Jesus, He asks us to take His yoke and put it on. In the days that Jesus spoke these words, everyone would have known what He was talking about when He referred to a yoke. Our modern world today is in-

---

110 Matthew 11:28
111 John 14:20
112 John 10:27
113 John 14:21
114 Revelation 3:20

creasingly unfamiliar with a yoke and what its purpose is. I'm old enough to have personally known people who farmed with horses, mules, or oxen before the introduction of motorized tractors. A yoke is a device for joining together two or more draft animals to pull a loaded wagon or farming implement. By joining two or more draft animals, you can pull heavier loads for longer distances with less effort. One of the key root words in *yoke* means "to join together." That's exactly what Jesus invites you to do. He wants you join to His yoke instead of you trying to pull your load all by yourself. And just like a strong big brother, Jesus ends up pulling most of the load!

When Jesus spoke these words recorded in Matthew 11, He was speaking to a crowd of people who had been so loaded down with religious rules and regulations that they could hardly bear the heavy load. For those who are still trying to live under the Old Covenant, that heavy burden still weighs them down. While most Christians have rightfully abandoned adherence to much of the Old Covenant Law, many are still unnecessarily carrying the burden of Sabbath laws from the Old Testament.

When you accept Jesus' invitation to take His yoke, every day is a day of sabbath rest. That doesn't mean that you'll never be physically tired or feel mentally fatigued. It also doesn't mean that you don't have to work! What it means is that you don't need to carry the additional burden in your soul of anxiety, chaos, fear, despair, anger, offense, and so on. When you quit trying to pull the load by yourself and let Jesus take these burdens, you will instantly feel more rested—physically, mentally, and emotionally.

Learn

After Jesus invites you to come to Him and take His yoke, He also invites you to learn from Him. It's important to note that He says to learn *from* Him rather than simply learn *about* Him. That's a big distinction. I can learn facts about a person, but those facts alone will do little to affect my life. If I learn *from* that same person, I'm able to implement what I've learned from them and use that information to bring about positive change in my life. It's the same with Jesus. He doesn't just want you to know about Him, He wants you to spend time with Him so that you can become more familiar with His character and nature, and how He operates. The more you understand Jesus, the more you'll come to trust Him in your everyday life, and the more likely you are to take His yoke and give Him your burdens.

The Best Rest

When I was in kindergarten, we had a fifteen-minute nap time every day. I don't think anyone ever actually napped, but the idea was to take a time of rest. At the end of each week, the teacher would give out the much-coveted "Best Rester" award. It was coveted because it was a gold star that she would pin on our shirts. We weren't very interested in actually being the best rester; we just wanted the gold star! Week after week I would roll out my little rug and try to lay as still as possible so that I could get the award. But week after week, much to my disappointment, the teacher would call someone else's name to come receive the award. Finally, late in the year, I got it! I'm not sure that I really earned it; I think Mrs. Carlson was just running out of students to give it to.

My point is this—I wasn't interested in resting; I was interested in winning the "Best Rester" award. That same mindset is prevalent in many Christians today who are trying to live under the requirements of the Old Testament Sabbath. They're more focused on "getting the award" than they are in actually getting some rest.

To be clear, the idea of a sabbath rest precedes the Old Covenant and is an important principle for us to follow today. If God rested from His work, how much more do we need to rest from ours? It's a godly practice to get adequate rest. But if you allow yourself to be put back under the yoke of bondage to the Law,[115] especially as it refers to the Sabbath, you'll not find the most important rest, which is rest for your soul.

The main theme of the book of Hebrews is that the New Covenant is superior to the Old Covenant in every way.[116] That means the sabbath rest under the New Covenant, found in the person of Jesus Christ, is superior to the Old Covenant Sabbath with all its rules and regulations. So, come into the presence of Jesus, and let Him pull your load so that you can find rest for your soul. Real rest.

---

115   Galatians 5:1
116   Hebrews 7:22

TORN

CHAPTER 13

A New Helper

Have you ever been in a difficult situation emotionally, spiritually, mentally, or even physically, and someone came alongside to help you? That's happened to me numerous times in my life, and probably to you, as well. But there have also been times in my life when I was struggling and no help seemed available. I felt as though I was on my own to sink or swim. Have you ever been in a place like that? Probably. Maybe you're in that place right now. If you are, I've got some great news for you.

Father God, at the request of His Son, Jesus, has sent you a Helper.

I will ask the Father, and He will give you another Helper, that He may be with you forever; that is the Spirit of truth, whom the world cannot receive, because it does not see Him or know Him, but you know Him because He abides with you and will be in you.
John 14:16-17 NASB

Jesus is referring here to the Holy Spirit, the third person of the Trinity and every bit divine as the Father and the Son. The word *Helper* in John 14:16 is translated from the Greek word *parakletos,* which basically means "one who comes alongside." That same word has also been translated as advocate, comforter, and counselor.

Jesus refers to the Holy Spirit as "He" rather than "it," because the Holy Spirit is a person. Even though God the Father is much different than us in many ways, we still refer to "Him" as a person. Thinking of Jesus as a person seems much easier, because He lived a human life here on earth. But for some reason, many believers have a hard time thinking of the Holy Spirit as a person. If we don't think of the Holy Spirit as a person, we could tend to view Him as some sort of impersonal cosmic force that would more closely align us to the New Age philosophy of positive energy.

In addition to the personal pronouns that refer to the Holy Spirit, the Bible also says that He experiences emotions.[117] Cosmic forces do not experience emotions—people do. People who are made in the image of God. Our God—Father, Son, and Holy Spirit—is a personal God who thinks, feels, and acts.

Even though Jesus said that the Father would be sending us the Holy Spirit, it's important to note that the Holy Spirit has always been here as part of the eternal Godhead. Before the New Covenant, the Holy Spirit would move through certain people at certain times to accomplish the will of God. As Jesus initiated the New Covenant, He said that the Holy Spirit would be available to every believer, at all times. This is a game-changer in the life of the believer and for the kingdom of God.

Our Helper[118]—who thinks, feels, and acts—is ready, willing, and able to help you at any time.

Helping You to Know the Truth

Jesus called the Holy Spirit the Spirit of Truth, because He reveals God's truth to us. As we connect with God through

117   Ephesians 4:30
118   John 14:16

Bible reading, prayer, and worship, the Holy Spirit is revealing truth to our hearts and minds. Even before we come to faith in Jesus, the Holy Spirit is speaking truth to us by convincing us of our sin and our need for a Savior.[119]

In my years as a pastor, helping people hear the voice of the God, I've found that many people are surprised at how easily they can hear from the Holy Spirit. Our problem is not that we don't hear the Holy Spirit speak truth to us. Our problem is *suppressing* that truth.[120] And if we continue to suppress God's truth, we ultimately end up exchanging the truth for a lie.[121] In other words, we begin to believe the lie as the truth, and the truth now becomes a lie. The reality of this delusion is increasingly evident in our world today.

Much of our unrest, both personally and in the world as a whole, comes from a lack of truth. Actually, there isn't really a lack of truth in our world—just a lack of people *following* the truth. Jesus said that He is the way, the *truth*, and the life.[122] He is also called the Prince of Peace.[123] When the angels announced His birth, they said that peace would come to those who walk in His grace.[124] Jesus even came right out and clearly told us that He came to give us peace as a gift.[125] If you connect the dots, you can see that it's the Holy Spirit that leads us into God's truth, and God's truth leads us into God's peace. So, if you're suppressing God's truth, you're suppressing God's peace.

It's time to take an honest look at yourself and ask your Helper if there are any areas in your life where you're suppressing God's truth. Are there any of God's truths that you have

---

119	John 16:8
120	Romans 1:18
121	Romans 1:25
122	John 14:6
123	Isaiah 9:6
124	Luke 2:14
125	John 14:27

exchanged for a lie? The good news is that your Helper can help you exchange a lie for the truth. The question is whether or not you're willing to hear the truth. I hope you are, because the *real* truth will set you free.

> **Then you will know the truth, and the truth will set you free.**
>
> **John 8:32 NIV**

For you to really be free, you need to know the truth. And to really know the truth you're going to need your Helper, because where the Spirit of the Lord is, there is freedom.[126]

Helping You to Live Righteously

Living righteously basically means doing what's right in the eyes of God. The opposite of living righteously, then, would be living sinfully. There's a tension in the lives of many Christians who know they are called to live righteously and yet struggle to do just that. If that sounds like you, you're not alone. In Romans 7, the apostle Paul writes about having the same struggle—wanting to live righteously, but not doing a very good job of it. Fortunately for us, Romans 7 is not the last chapter of the book. Instead of throwing up his hands and telling us there's nothing we can do, Paul goes on in chapter 8 to tell us that the answer to this struggle is found in the Holy Spirit. In his letter to the Galatians, Paul gives more clarity to this truth:

> **So I say, walk by the Spirit, and you will not gratify the desires of the flesh.**
>
> **Galatians 5:16 NIV**

126   2 Corinthians 3:17

To walk by the Spirit means to listen to the voice of the Holy Spirit as He speaks to your heart, and then to actually do what He says. Your Helper doesn't put a collar on you and then drag you wherever He wants you to go. Instead, your Helper comes alongside you and speaks truth to you so you can choose the proper course of action. As long as you do what He says you will live righteously, but if you suppress His voice you are very likely to wander off in sin.

You may recall from what you read previously in this book that the main idea of the New Covenant is that the Holy Spirit would write God's laws on our hearts[127] instead of on tablets of stone. We no longer need to follow a set of written rules, because now our Helper speaks directly to our hearts. As New Covenant believers, the key to living righteous and holy lives is not by trying to follow a bunch of written rules and regulations, but rather by following the leading of the Holy Spirit.

> **But when you are directed by the Spirit, you are not under obligation to the law of Moses.**
> **Galatians 5:18 NLT**

Helping You to Be Comforted

As I stated earlier in this chapter, the Greek word *parakletos* has sometimes been translated as "comforter." Jesus knew that in this life we would need comforting, so He asked the Father to send the Comforter. Because sin runs rampant in our world, people are going to get hurt. Sin causes a lot of collateral damage. Even though the blood of Jesus washes our sins away when we turn to Him, the scars and bruises left behind from that sin need to be healed. When we allow the Comforter

127   Jeremiah 31:33

into our lives He can bring soothing relief to our deepest hurts, even when those hurts are self-inflicted.

The physical death of a loved one and the ensuing grief is something most of us have experienced. The shortest verse in the Bible conveys the grief Jesus experienced when His friend Lazarus died.[128] The Holy Spirit doesn't take our grief away, because it's an appropriate and necessary emotion when we suffer profound loss. He does, however, console and soothe us during our period of grief.

> **Praise be to the God and Father of our Lord Jesus Christ, the Father of compassion and the God of all comfort, who comforts us in all our troubles, so that we can comfort those in any trouble with the comfort we ourselves receive from God.**
> **2 Corinthians 1:3-4 NIV**

When we're going through difficult times, we may be fortunate enough to have a friend or spouse who knows just how to bring some measure of comfort to our situation. But honestly, for many people, this is seldom the case. Most of the people who are close to us want to give us comfort in our distress, but they just don't know how to do it. But our Helper—our Comforter—knows exactly how to do it. You just need to receive it.

Helping You to Help Others

One characteristic about God that became evident through Jesus is His compassion toward people. It's His desire that we, too, would have compassion on those around us. While there are many practical ways in which we can minister to those around us, I want to focus on those ways in which only an empowered Christian can minister to others. Let me put it another way. If we see that someone is hungry, we should

---

128   John 11:35

feed them. If we see that someone needs clothing, we should clothe them. If we see that someone is homeless, we should give them shelter. But the truth is, atheists can do this just a well as Christians. We, as followers of Jesus, should help others in these practical ways just mentioned, but we shouldn't stop there. You, as a follower of Jesus, are empowered by the Holy Spirit to help others in ways that no one else can.

In the New Covenant, Jesus gave us a clear mandate to share His gospel of the kingdom to all people.[129] But He also told us not to attempt this until we received empowerment from the Holy Spirit.[130]

> **But you will receive power when the Holy Spirit comes on you; and you will be my witnesses in Jerusalem, and in all Judea and Samaria, and to the ends of the earth.**
> **Acts 1:8 NIV**

So, what does this power look like as we serve others in our everyday life? To answer this question, let me illustrate it by putting you into a hypothetical situation. Let's say you're a delivery person, and you've been given a package to deliver. The contents of this package will forever change the life of the recipient in a very positive way. Do you deliver the package? Of course, you do! And since this is such an important package, you would take your assignment very seriously. You would also probably take great joy as the recipient receives this life-changing package. It almost makes you want to become a delivery person, doesn't it? Well, the fact of the matter is that you are. You are a delivery person for God the Holy Spirit.

In his first letter to the Corinthians, Paul says that he doesn't want us to be uninformed about what he calls the *gifts*

---

129   Matthew 24:14, Matthew 28:19
130   Luke 24:49

of the Spirit.[131] While different gifts of the Spirit are listed here and there in the New Testament, the most comprehensive list is found in 1 Corinthians 12:

> **Now to each one the manifestation of the Spirit is given for the common good. To one there is given through the Spirit a message of wisdom, to another a message of knowledge by means of the same Spirit, to another faith by the same Spirit, to another gifts of healing by that one Spirit, to another miraculous powers, to another prophecy, to another distinguishing between spirits, to another speaking in different kinds of tongues, and to still another the interpretation of tongues. All these are the work of one and the same Spirit, and he distributes them to each one, just as he determines.**
>
> **1 Corinthians 12:7-11 NIV**

Paul says that these gifts are a manifestation of the Holy Spirit. To *manifest* means to "make something visible." So, a manifestation of the Holy Spirit is when His supernatural power becomes visible through the gifts that are listed in 1 Corinthians 12. Furthermore, the Holy Spirit uses followers of Jesus to make these gifts visible at just the right time, and in just the right place. To do that, He needs you.

I've met more than a few Christians who think that the Holy Spirit gives them just one gift, and that they should seek to find that one gift and then show it off to the world. What they don't understand is that the gifts of the Spirit are rarely for you. They're almost always for someone else, and your responsibility is to deliver the gift to the person who needs it. When you're in need of one of these spiritual gifts for yourself, the Holy Spirit will gladly give it to you. But generally speak-

---

131   1 Corinthians 12:1

ing, you don't keep the gift—you deliver it when and where the Holy Spirit tells you to. As a follower of Jesus, you should be ready, willing, and able to deliver any and all of the nine gifts of the Spirit as your Helper directs you.

> **Each of you should use whatever gift you have received to serve others, as faithful stewards of God's grace in its various forms.**
> **1 Peter 4:10 NIV**

There are many ways in which you can help people that don't require supernatural empowerment from God, and you should do those things. However, there are things God wants to do for His people that can only be accomplished through Spirit-filled believers such as yourself. You have the privilege and the responsibility to deliver gifts from the Holy Spirit to those who need them, and your Helper is right there to talk you through every step. Listen to Him.

Helping You to Pray

As a Christian, you've probably been in a situation or a season when you didn't even know how you should pray. Maybe the situation was so complex that you didn't know what to pray for. Or maybe you prayed so much that you didn't know what else there was that you could possibly pray about. Perhaps you had very little information about the situation you were praying for and felt as though your prayer was overly generalized, and therefore maybe not as effective as it could be. I have good news for all of you who have struggled with how to pray in certain situations. Your Helper can pray a laser-targeted prayer for you and through you.

> **In the same way the Spirit also helps our weakness;**
> **for we do not know how to pray as we should, but the**
> **Spirit Himself intercedes for us with groanings too deep**
> **for words.**
>
> **Romans 8:26 NASB**

While there are differing interpretations on what "groanings too deep for words" could mean, it's very clear from this verse that the Holy Spirit prays on our behalf. That could mean that our Helper speaks a perfect prayer on our behalf to God the Father without us even knowing He's doing it. Although that could be the case, Paul sheds some light on how this could all happen.

In 1 Corinthians 12, Paul tells us about the supernatural gifts of the Holy Spirit that are available for us to use to help others. In chapter 14, he rebukes the members of the church in Corinth for their abuse of these gifts. He goes to great lengths to teach them how the gifts of the Spirit are to be used in a public church setting, because he knows they play an important role in the mission of the local church. Intermingled with his teaching on supernatural gifts in the church, Paul also talks about praying in tongues as a personal prayer language to God. He differentiates the use of tongues as a way of personal prayer from speaking in tongues with interpretation in a public setting.

> **For anyone who speaks in a tongue does not speak to**
> **people but to God. Indeed, no one understands them; they**
> **utter mysteries by the Spirit.**
>
> **1 Corinthians 14:2 NIV**

What's so awesome about privately praying to God in tongues is that even though you don't know what you're saying, your Helper is speaking the perfect prayer through you in a language that the Father understands.

> **For if I pray in tongues, my spirit is praying, but I don't understand what I am saying. Well then, what shall I do? I will pray in the spirit, and I will also pray in words I understand. I will sing in the spirit, and I will also sing in words I understand.**
>
> **1 Corinthians 14:14-15 NLT**

There are times when it's best to pray in our native tongue, but there are also times when it's best to pray in a language unknown to us. The best way I've found to enter into this powerful prayer mode is to begin by praying out loud in English. I continue to speak, but at some point, I let my mouth start to speak words that are unintelligible to me. Although this may not sound very spiritual to you, this is where you launch out and just let the sounds and syllables come without your analysis. At this point, you have given control of your mouth to the Holy Spirit, and even though you don't know what you're saying, God the Father is understanding you completely. This is how the Holy Spirit prays the perfect prayer through you. The Bible refers to this in several places in the New Testament as "praying in the Spirit."[132]

For several months after I had discovered the biblical truth about praying in the Spirit, I waited and waited for this experience to happen to me. I thought that as I sat in quiet expectation, the Holy Spirit would suddenly cause me to erupt in a flurry of tongue-speaking that I could hardly control. While this may have happened to some people, it's certainly not my story.

I grew up in a mainline liturgical church where prayers

---

132   Jude 20

were almost always recited from a printed document, whether it be the weekly bulletin or the book of worship. While this type of prayer didn't really resonate with me, it did teach me the value of praying out loud. Praying silently to God can be very powerful and is probably the way I most often pray. However, you don't speak in tongues with your mind—you speak in tongues with your voice. If I had waited during my silent prayer time for the Holy Spirit to begin speaking through me, I'd still be waiting. At some point you actually have to open your mouth, vibrate your vocal cords, and move your tongue if you want to pray in tongues. This simple revelation forever changed my prayer life.

Praising God and praying to Him vocally used to be very uncomfortable to me, and maybe to you as well. But at some point, you've got to get over yourself. If you want to pray laser-targeted prayers through the Holy Spirit by praying in tongues, you'll need to start by praying in English. As you begin to form non-English words it may just sound like gibberish to you, but you have to trust the Holy Spirit. As you push through those first few uncomfortable seconds of speaking in tongues, you'll find that pretty quickly the words will begin to flow more fluently.

If this all sounds a little weird to you, I understand. When God moves in power, it can often seem a little weird. In Christianity there's "good" weird and "bad" weird. When people willfully handle poisonous snakes just to make a show of their faith—that's bad weird. When people shave their heads, put on white robes, and go stand on the hill out of town to wait for Jesus to come get them—that's bad weird. Two times in my life, so far, I've prayed for people with visibly broken bones and watched as those bones popped back into place and were instantly healed. That was weird. Good weird. Godly people, through the gifting of the Holy Spirit, have spoken a word of knowledge[133] to me with intimate details that they could have never known on their own. That was weird. Good weird. Do you get my point? Just because something is weird or seems strange doesn't mean it's not from God. Speaking in an unknown language through the power of the Holy Spirit to pray perfect prayers to God is weird. Good weird.

Many of you reading this book have been praying in the Spirit for a long time. For others, this is a new concept. And yet I know, from personal experience, that many of you have avoided this topic because you have been taught that praying in tongues is not for believers today. The problem with this teaching is that it can't be found in the Bible. Nowhere—unless you're willing to break almost every law of interpreting the Bible.

I encourage you to step out of your comfort zone and start praying in the Spirit with the help of your Helper. You need these perfect prayers. Your friends and family need these perfect prayers. The world needs these perfect prayers.

---

133   1 Corinthians 12:8

CHAPTER 14

A New Glory

During the time of the Old Covenant, the manifestation of God's glory was not an uncommon experience. One of my favorite accounts of God's glory being experienced by mankind was when King Solomon built the first temple. After the priests brought the Ark of the Covenant into the Most Holy Place, the glory of God fell so heavily that the priests could not continue their service.[134] All they could do was to fall before God in His glorious presence. While God's glory is multi-faceted, it could basically be defined as "the reverent and weighty presence of God's splendor." That definition of glory is clearly illustrated in this biblical account.

The word *glory* is found many places in the Bible and is used frequently in most Christian worship services. Whether in ancient hymns or contemporary worship music, the subject of God's glory abounds. But for all our preaching and singing about God's glory, how many Christians even know what His glory is? More importantly, how many Christians have ever encountered God's glory? How about you? Have you ever personally experienced a manifestation of God's glory that even comes close to what was experienced by believers in the Old Testament? Is it even biblical for you to experience God's glory like they did in the Old Testament?

Even though I personally know several believers that have experienced (and continue to experience) a powerful manifestation of God's glory, it would be my guess that most Chris-

---

134   1 Kings 8:10-11

tians do not. It would also be my guess that a large percentage of Christians don't think that such an experience is even available to us today. If that's you, I've got some exciting news. Not only can we expect God's glory to fall much like it did during the Old Covenant, but God's Word says that as New Covenant believers we should see even *more* dramatic encounters of God's glory.

The old way, with laws etched in stone, led to death, though it began with such glory that the people of Israel could not bear to look at Moses' face. For his face shone with the glory of God, even though the brightness was already fading away. Shouldn't we expect far greater glory under the new way, now that the Holy Spirit is giving life?
2 Corinthians 3:7-8 NLT

Moses and God's Glory

As God was establishing the Old Covenant (the Law), He spent two forty-day periods with Moses on Mount Sinai. It was during their second visit when Moses asked God to show him His glory.

Then Moses said, "Now show me your glory." And the Lord said, "I will cause all my goodness to pass in front of you, and I will proclaim my name, the Lord, in your presence."
Exodus 33:18-19 NIV

For many years I assumed that when Moses asked God to show him His glory, God's answer was basically, "I can't do that for you, but I'll show you My goodness instead."

But if you carefully read these verses, God didn't tell Moses anything of the sort. I, and I'm sure many others, just assumed that God's glory and God's goodness are two different things.

But in reality, God's goodness is a major aspect of His glory. In other words, when you experience God's glory, you experience God's goodness. With that in mind, it totally changes how we interpret God's answer to Moses. God *did* show Moses His glory when He showed Moses His goodness. Keep this important truth in mind, because later in this chapter I'm going to show you how God is still answering this request in your life today. Now, back to our story.

When Moses returned from his second visit with God on Mount Sinai, his face was so radiant that it actually scared the people who saw him.[135] After he got them settled back down, he spoke to them.

When Moses finished speaking to them, he put a veil over his face. But whenever he entered the Lord's presence to speak with him, he removed the veil until he came out. And when he came out and told the Israelites what he had been commanded, they saw that his face was radiant. Then Moses would put the veil back over his face until he went in to speak with the Lord.

Exodus 34:33-35 NIV

So, what's with all the veiling and unveiling of Moses' face? From what we read here in the Old Testament, Moses would remove the veil when he met with God in the tent of meeting and then go out and speak to the people with an unveiled face. For some reason, he would put the veil over his face after he was done speaking. But why? If the people were so weirded-out because of his overly radiant face, why didn't he wear the veil when he spoke to them? Wouldn't that make more sense? If we only read the Old Testament account, we can't really understand why Moses was repeatedly veiling and unveiling his face. Fortunately, the Holy Spirit revealed this reason to Paul, and he wrote about it in his second letter to the church in Corinth.

135   Exodus 34:29-31

We are not like Moses, who would put a veil over his face to prevent the Israelites from seeing the end of what was passing away.

2 Corinthians 3:13 NIV

The longer Moses was away from the glorious presence of God, the more the radiance in his face would fade. Apparently, Moses didn't want the people to see that, so that's why he veiled his face. Even though his unveiled, radiant face unnerved those who saw him, it at least got their attention.

It didn't dawn on me until recently that this whole episode was a prophetic illustration that the covenant God was making with Moses and the people—what we now refer to as the Old Covenant—was only temporary. We know from reading elsewhere in the Bible that the Old Covenant was temporary, but the veiled face of Moses illustrates that truth in a way I hadn't seen before. The temporary nature of God's glorious radiance in the face of Moses represents the temporary nature of the Old Covenant. It was destined to fade. God's glory was undeniably manifested in the Old Covenant, but that glory has faded away. That's one reason why people who still try to live under the Old Covenant today may lack any significant personal experience of God's glory.

God's Glory in the New Covenant

Many years ago, when I was still trying to live in both the Old and New Covenants, I remember reading in the Bible about the amazing manifestations of God's glory in the Old Testament and thinking how amazing it would have been to witness something like that. What I didn't know at the time is that God's Word says that as believers living under the New Covenant, we should experience even *more* of God's glory!

Shouldn't we expect far greater glory under the new way, now that the Holy Spirit is giving life?

2 Corinthians 3:8 NLT

Under the Old Covenant God's glory grew dimmer and dimmer, but under the New Covenant God's glory grows brighter and brighter, because of the ministry of the Holy Spirit in our lives.

Another important prophetic illustration of Moses' veil gives us a key to experiencing God's manifest glory under the New Covenant. It pertains to the veil (curtain) in the temple that separated the Most Holy Place—the dwelling place of God—from the rest of the temple. Only the high priest could go beyond the temple veil, and only once a year was he permitted to enter the Most Holy Place. Moses' veil was a prophetic representation of the veil in the Old Covenant tabernacle and temple that separated man from the personal presence of God. So, here's the key: Moses always removed his veil when he entered the tent of meeting to speak with God, because there could be no curtain separating them. Likewise, if we're going to experience the glorious presence of God, there can be no veil between Him and us. Furthermore, in order to radiate the glory of God, we need to meet with Him face-to-face, spiritually speaking.

But we all, with unveiled face, beholding as in a mirror the glory of the Lord, are being transformed into the same image from glory to glory, just as from the Lord, the Spirit.

2 Corinthians 3:18 NASB

To have a veiled face means to still be stuck in Old Covenant law and have the guilty conscience that comes with it. The book of Hebrews tells us that even though the Old Covenant made provisions for our sins to be covered until Jesus came, it could never give us a clear conscience.[136] One thing that's clear in the Bible is that people who have a guilty conscience are highly unlikely to have the desire to come into the presence of God.

At the risk of offending people by comparing us to dogs, let me use this illustration. I, like many of you, have a pet dog. Whenever I come home, no matter how long I've been gone, my dog excitedly greets me and wants to be as close to me as possible. However, I can always tell when I come home if she's gotten into something she shouldn't have. Instead of meeting me at the door with love and kisses, she'll be slinking around with downcast eyes, knowing that she's in trouble for making a mess. She makes every effort to avoid me as much as possible. Again, no offense please, but it's a very similar situation between us and God when we're attempting to live under the Old Covenant. Our guilty conscience keeps us from entering into the presence of God.

Thankfully, under the New Covenant, the blood of Jesus takes our sin away and gives us a clear conscience so that we can confidently enter into the glorious presence of God.

Therefore, brothers and sisters, since we have confidence to enter the Most Holy Place by the blood of Jesus, by a new and living way opened for us through the curtain, that is, his body, and since we have a great priest over the house of God, let us draw near to God with a sincere heart and with the full assurance that faith brings, having our hearts sprinkled to cleanse us from a guilty conscience and having our bodies washed with pure water.
Hebrews 10:19-22 NIV

---

136   Hebrews 9:9

Changed by God's Glory

As we unveil our face and come into God's presence, we can't help but be changed. In 1 Corinthians 3:18, Paul uses the word *transformed* as he describes what happens to us when the eyes of our hearts[137] gaze upon the face of God. The word *transformed*, in the original language of the New Testament (Greek), is the same root word as our English word for metamorphosis. Just as a lowly caterpillar is transformed into a beautiful butterfly, we're continually being transformed to radiate more and more of God's glory. And that transformation can only happen in the presence of God. Thousands of years of biblical history have shown us that behavior modification and self-effort are not very effective in transforming our lives to more closely resemble the image of God. What has proven effective, however, is being in the manifest presence of God.

When your life is transformed by being in God's glorious presence, it's certainly an awesome thing. As you radiate the glory of God, people around you may also begin to change. Even though Moses' radiant face initially alarmed the people, they were at least intrigued and eventually came in closer to hear what he had to say. It gave Moses credibility as he shared God's life-giving words with the people. The same thing will happen to you. Even though your face may not be physically illuminated like Moses' was, you will radiate God's glory in a way that will get people's attention. It may be subtle, but as you spend more time in the personal presence of God, people will begin to notice. They'll notice that you have peace in times of chaos. They'll notice that you have hope when everyone around you is hopeless. They'll notice that you have joy, regardless of your circumstances. They'll notice that when you walk into the room, the atmosphere begins to change. Eventually, most of them will want what you have. And what you have is the glorious presence of God in your life.

Are you radiating the glorious presence of God? You may be wondering how you would know if you are or not. Here's how you will know: People will tell you. Most people won't

---

137   Ephesians 1:18

walk up to you and say, "Wow! You've got God's glorious presence all over you!" But they will notice that things are different about you. And eventually, they'll begin to mention it. At some point, many of them will ask you how they can have what you have.

By the way, if you have to tell people that you're radiating the glory of God to get them to notice, you're probably not radiating all that much. If it's real, people will notice. If it's something you're trying to manufacture, they'll notice that, too. Just not in a good way. If you want to radiate the glory of God, you've got to spend time in the presence of God.

Where to Look for God's Glory

Hopefully, by now, you're excited to experience the glory of God and let it transform your life and the lives of those around you. But where do you start? Where do you go to find the glory of God? Fortunately, God's Word tells you exactly where to look.

**For God, who said, "Let there be light in the darkness,"
has made this light shine in our hearts so we could know
the glory of God that is seen in the face of Jesus Christ.**
2 Corinthians 4:6 NLT

Boom. There it is. You'll find the glory of God in the face of Jesus. You don't see the face of Jesus with your physical eyes; you see Him with your spiritual eyes. In what seems to be a paradox, the Bible tells us not to look at what is seen, but rather to look at what is not seen.[138] In other words, we should quit focusing all our attention on the natural world and start focusing on the spiritual realm, because that's where we'll see Jesus. Jesus even promised us that He would show Himself to us.

---

138   2 Corinthians 4:18

Whoever has my commands and keeps them is the one who loves me. The one who loves me will be loved by my Father, and I too will love them and show myself to them.

John 14:21 NIV

One of the most amazing things you'll ever experience is a life that has been transformed by the power and presence of Jesus Christ. Self-help won't do it. Behavior modification won't do it. Trying harder won't do it. But experiencing the manifest glory of God *will* do it. You just have to know where to look. If you look to the Law of the Old Covenant, you won't find it. But if you look into the face of Jesus, you *will* find it—and it will change your life forever.